WRITING EMPIRICAL RESEARCH REPORTS

A Basic Guide for Students of
the Social and Behavioral Sciences

Fred Pyrczak

California State University, Los Angeles

Randall R. Bruce

Editorial Consultant

Pyrczak Publishing
P.O. Box 39731
Los Angeles, CA 90039

ISBN 0–9623744–3–1

CONTENTS

INTRODUCTION

This book presents principles frequently followed by writers of reports of empirical research designed for publication in academic journals. The principles describe the types of information that should be included, how this information should be expressed, and where various types of information should be placed within a report.

Students whose professors require them to write research-based term papers that resemble journal articles will find this book useful. The exercises at the end of each chapter are designed for use by students in such classes.

Graduate students who are writing theses and dissertations will find that most of the principles also apply to their writing. Interspersed throughout the text are pointers for such students.

Students who are writing research proposals also will find that most of the principles apply to their writing.

What this Book Will *Not* Do for You

This book is not a traditional style manual that prescribes mechanical details such as how to cite references, the forms for levels of headings, typing requirements, and so forth. Excellent style manuals that already do this are described in Appendix D.

Nor will you find here a discussion of the mechanics of standard English usage; it is assumed that you have already mastered these.

Finally, it is assumed that you have already selected a significant research topic, applied sound research methods, and analyzed the data. Thus, these topics are not covered.

Cautions in Using this Book

The principles suggested in this book are based on generalizations that we reached while reading extensively in journals in the social and behavioral sciences. If you are a student using this book in a research class, your professor may ask you to ignore or modify some of the principles you will find here. This may occur for two reasons. First, as a learning experience, your professor may require you to do certain things that go beyond the preparation of a paper for possible publication. For example, we suggest that the literature review for a journal article usually should be highly selective; your professor may wish to have you write a more extensive literature review in order to have you demonstrate that you know how to locate literature and to demonstrate your breadth of knowledge of the topic on which you have done research. Second, as in all types of writing, there is a certain amount of subjectivity as to what constitutes effective writing; even experts differ. Fortunately, these differences are less pronounced in scientific writing than in many other types.

Experienced writers of research may violate many of the principles presented here and still write effective research reports that are publishable. Beginners are encouraged to follow the principles rather closely until they have mastered the art of scientific writing.

About the Appendices

Appendix A provides a checklist of the principles described in this book. This should be used while writing and revising reports. The principles in this appendix are sequentially numbered. While reviewing students' work, professors may wish to refer to these numbers in their written comments on research reports (e.g., "See Principle 5.2 in Appendix A").

Appendices B and C contain essays on effective research report writing. We believe that they present important principles that are consistent with the philosophy underlying this book.

Appendix D provides a highly selective list of suggested readings, software, and videotapes.

Acknowledgements

The authors are grateful to Dr. Dean Purcell of Oakland University and to two anonymous reviewers who provided helpful comments on the first draft of this manuscript. We are also indebted to Holbrook Mahn, Patricia A. Steele, and Robert Morman for their editorial assistance.

Chapter 1

WRITING SIMPLE RESEARCH HYPOTHESES

In a single sentence, a simple research hypothesis describes the results that a researcher expects to find. In effect, it is a prediction. The following are principles for writing this type of hypothesis.

✔ **Principle 1: A simple research hypothesis should name two variables and indicate the type of relationship expected between them.**

Example 1-A: There is a positive relationship between level of psychomotor coordination and degree of self-esteem.

In Example 1-A, the variables are "psychomotor coordination" and "self-esteem." The researcher expects to find higher self-esteem among subjects who have more psychomotor coordination and lower self-esteem among those who have less coordination. Note that the word "direct" may be substituted for "positive" without changing the meaning of the hypothesis.

Example 1-B: Length of light deprivation from birth among rats is inversely associated with performance in a maze task.

In Example 1-B, "length of light deprivation" is an independent or stimulus variable; its relationship to "performance in a maze task" is stated in the hypothesis—the longer the period of deprivation, the worse the performance in a maze task.

Example 1-C: Teachers who are given a paper on practical tips for mainstreaming learning disabled students will be more willing to have such students in their classrooms than teachers who are given a theoretical paper on learning disabilities.

1

Example 1-C also contains an independent variable — the type of paper given to teachers. The anticipated relationship to the willingness of teachers to accept learning disabled students is clear in the hypothesis. This willingness is known as the outcome or dependent variable.

Example 1-D: College students differ in their levels of free-floating anxiety, and they differ in their ability to form friendships.

In Example 1-D, two variables are named but the expected relationship between them is not stated. The Improved Version of Example 1-D makes it clear that the author believes that those with more free-floating anxiety have less ability to form friendships.

Improved Version of Example 1-D: There is an inverse relationship between level of free-floating anxiety and ability to form friendships among college students.

In the Improved Version of Example 1-D, the word "negative" could be substituted for "inverse" without changing the meaning of the hypothesis.

✔ **Principle 2: When a relationship is expected only among a certain type of subject, reference to the population should be made in the hypothesis.**

Example 2-A: Among young children, there is a positive relationship between level of psychomotor coordination and degree of self-esteem.

In Example 2-A, young children are identified as the population of interest to the investigator.

✔ **Principle 3: A simple hypothesis should be as specific as possible yet expressed in a single sentence.** For example, the meanings of "computer literacy" and "computer use" are clearer in the improved version than in the original version of Example 3-A.

> **Example 3-A:** There is a direct relationship between administrators' computer literacy and computer use.

> **Improved Version of Example 3-A:** Among administrators, there is a direct relationship between the amount of training they have had in the use of computers and the number of administrative tasks they perform using computers.

A certain amount of subjectivity enters into the decision on how specific to make a hypothesis. It is often not possible to provide fully operational definitions (i.e., definitions that fully describe the physical attributes of a variable) in a hypothesis. These definitions should be provided elsewhere in a research paper. Principles for writing definitions are presented in Chapter 6.

> **Example 3-B:** Administrators who provide wellness programs for their employees project positive effectiveness.

In Example 3-B, "positive effectiveness" is vague. This flaw is partially corrected in the improved version.

> **Improved Version of Example 3-B:** Administrators who provide wellness programs for their employees receive higher employee ratings on selected leadership qualities than administrators who do not provide wellness programs.

The Improved Version of Example 3-B indicates that "effectiveness" will be defined in terms of employee perceptions. The "selected leadership qualities" and "wellness programs" will need to be more fully defined elsewhere in the research paper.

✔ **Principle 4: If a comparison is to be made, the elements to be compared should be stated.**

> **Example 4-A:** Younger children are more dependent on adults for psychological support.

> **Improved Version of Example 4-A:** Younger children are more dependent on adults for psychological support than older children.

In the Improved Version of Example 4-A, the fact that younger children are to be compared with older children is clear.

✔ **Principle 5: Because most hypotheses deal with the behavior of groups, plural forms should usually be used.**

> **Example 5-A:** There is a direct relationship between a nurse's participation in administrative decision making and her level of job satisfaction.

In Example 5-A, the terms "nurse's" and "her level" are singular. This problem has been corrected in the improved version by substituting the terms "nurses'" and "their level."

> **Improved Version of Example 5-A:** There is a direct relationship between nurses' participation in administrative decision making and their level of job satisfaction.

In the Improved Version of Example 5-A, the sex-role stereotype regarding nurses has been eliminated. It is important, of course, to avoid sex-role stereotyping throughout research papers.

✔ **Principle 6: A hypothesis should be free of terms and phrases that do not add to its meaning.**

Example 6-A: Among elementary school teachers, those who are teaching in year-round schools will report having higher morale than those who are teaching in elementary schools that follow a more traditional school-year schedule.

Improved Version of Example 6-A: Among elementary school teachers, those who teach in year-round schools have higher morale than those who teach on a traditional schedule.

The Improved Version of Example 6-A is much shorter than the original version, yet its meaning is clear.

✔ **Principle 7: A hypothesis should indicate what will actually be studied — not the possible implications of the study or value judgments of the author.**

Example 7-A: The liberalization of Americans' attitudes on social issues will take a dramatic turn when baby boomers reach retirement age.

Because the hypothesis in Example 7-A cannot be tested within a reasonable time frame, it probably is a statement of possible implications.

Improved Version of Example 7-A: Retired Americans have more conservative attitudes on social issues than baby boomers.

The Improved Version of Example 7-A probably reflects more accurately the methodology that the author plans to use. If the hypothesis is supported by data, the author may wish to speculate in the discussion section of the report that, in the future, the current generation of baby boomers may become more like currently retired people.

Example 7-B: Religion is good for society.

In Example 7-B, the author is expressing a value judgment rather than describing the anticipated relationship between the variables to be studied. The improved version more clearly indicates how "religion" will be treated as a variable and indicates the actual outcome, "cheating behavior," that will be measured.

Improved Version of Example 7-B: Regular attendance at religious services is inversely associated with cheating behavior while taking classroom tests.

If the hypothesis is supported by data, the writer may wish to assert that less cheating is "good" for society in the introduction to the research report or in the discussion section; such an assertion would be acceptable as long as it is clear from the context that the author recognizes the assertion as a value judgment and not as a data-based conclusion.

✔ **Principle 8: A hypothesis usually should name variables in the order in which they occur or will be measured.**

Example 8-A: More free-floating anxiety will be observed among adults who are subjected to longer periods of sensory deprivation.

In Example 8-A, the natural order has been reversed because the deprivation will precede and possibly produce the anticipated anxiety.

Improved Version of Example 8-A: Adults who are subjected to extended periods of sensory deprivation will experience more free-floating anxiety than those exposed to less deprivation.

Example 8-B: There is a positive relationship between first-semester grades earned in college and College Board Scholastic Aptitude Test scores.

Because College Boards are normally taken prior to entry into college, reference to them should be made before reference to freshman grades, as in the Improved Version of Example 8-B.

> **Improved Version of Example 8-B:** There is a positive relationship between College Board Scholastic Aptitude Test scores and first-semester grades earned in college.

✔ **Principle 9: Avoid using the words "significant" or "significance" in a hypothesis.** These terms usually refer to the results of tests of statistical significance. Because most empirical studies include tests of statistical significance, inclusion of these terms in a hypothesis is not necessary; sophisticated readers will assume that the results of significance tests will probably be reported in the results section of the research paper.

✔ **Principle 10: Avoid using the word "prove" in a hypothesis.** Empirical research relies on observations or measurements that are less than perfectly reliable; they usually involve only samples from a population; furthermore, there may be biases in procedures. For these reasons, errors are almost always present in the results of empirical studies. Thus, we cannot deduct a conclusive proof, as one might in mathematics, by using the empirical method.

✔ **Principle 11: Avoid using two different terms to refer to the same variable.**

> **Example 11-A:** Students who receive a literature-based approach to reading instruction plus training in phonetics will have better attitudes toward reading than those who receive only the new approach to reading instruction.

In Example 11-A, it is not clear whether the "new approach" is the literature-based approach or some other new approach. This problem is corrected in the Improved Version of Example 11-A.

> **Improved Version of Example 11-A:** Students who receive a literature-based approach to reading instruction plus training in phonetics will have better attitudes toward reading than those who receive only a literature-based approach.

EXERCISE FOR CHAPTER 1

The following questions are provided for review and classroom discussion. Because the application of many of the principles involves a certain amount of subjectivity, there may be some legitimate differences of opinion on the best answers to some of the questions.

PART A: Name the two variables in each of the following hypotheses.

1. Middle socio-economic status (SES) students participate in more extracurricular activities than low SES students.

2. Teachers who are skilled at building positive interpersonal relationships with other teachers are perceived by their administrators as being more effective in communicating information to their students than teachers who are less skilled in building such relationships.

3. Among college graduates, authoritarianism and anxiety are directly related.

4. Children who are shown a film with numerous instances of physical violence will demonstrate more aggressiveness during a free play period than children who are shown a control film without violence.

PART B: For each of the following hypotheses, name the principle(s), if any, that were not applied. Revise each hypothesis that you think is faulty. In your revisions, you may need to make some assumptions about what the authors had in mind when writing the hypotheses.

5. ~~The hypothesis is to prove that~~ first-born boys have a greater desire to achieve high grades in the primary grades than second-born boys have.

6. Children differ in age and they also differ in their ability to attend to instructional presentations. *Younger children are less able to attend to instruc pres than older children*

7. The rate of development of speech in young children is directly related to the verbal fluency of their parents.

8. Among high achievers, there will be a higher level of sibling rivalry. *than among lower achievers*

9. ~~Other things being equal,~~ the greater the number of rewards, *verbal a person receives* the better the performance. *at school*

10. There is a direct relationship between a mechanical engineer's ability to visualize objects rotating in space and his success on the job.

11. The social agenda of the present administration is weak.

12. Among college applicants, there will be less test-taking anxiety among those who take a test-preparation course. *than those applicants who do not take the test prep course.*

13. There will be a significant relationship between age and height. *In high school sts there is an inversely direct relationship between age and height as compared with primary grade sts.*

14. Students who take Psychology I will report greater self-insight than students who do not take Introductory Psychology.

15. Different subcultures view the school environment differently.

PART C: Write a simple hypothesis on a topic of interest to you. Include in the hypothesis a reference to a population. Underline the names of the two variables.

NOTES

10

Chapter 2

A CLOSER LOOK AT HYPOTHESES

This chapter presents some advanced principles for writing hypotheses and explores some of the principles from Chapter 1 in more detail.

✔ **Principle 1: A "statement of the hypotheses" may contain more than one hypothesis. It is permissible to include them in a single sentence as long as the sentence is reasonably concise and its meaning is clear.**

> **Example 1-A:** Clients experiencing mild levels of depression will report more relief from their symptoms and greater satisfaction with the counseling process when individual therapy is supplemented with group therapy.

In Example 1-A, there is one independent variable (supplementary group therapy) and two anticipated outcomes or dependent variables. Therefore, there are two hypotheses: (1) those who receive the group therapy supplement will report more relief and (2) those who receive the group therapy supplement will be more satisfied.

Note that in Example 1-A, the reader must infer that there probably will be a comparison or control group that will not receive group therapy because the comparison that begins with "greater" has not been completed. This violation of Principle 4 in Chapter 1 is sometimes found in published research. However, it would be desirable to end the hypothesis with the phrase "than clients who receive only individual therapy."

✔ **Principle 2: When a number of related hypotheses are to be stated, consider presenting them in a numbered or lettered list.**

Example 2-A presents part of a list presented by Pultzer (1988, p. 641).

> **Example 2-A:** "From the literature reviewed, I derived four major hypotheses . . .
> HYPOTHESIS 1. Women's family life is related to support of feminist goals with
> a. The divorced and never married more feminist than those who are married or widowed, and
> b. The number of children negatively associated with feminist attitudes.
> HYPOTHESIS 2. Women's employment status and experience is related to support of feminist goals with
> a. Women in the labor force more feminist than all others,
> b. Women who have never worked most traditional,
> c. The number of hours worked positively associated with feminism . . . ."

There are five specific hypotheses in Example 2-A, organized under two major hypotheses. Evidence regarding the major hypotheses will be obtained by testing the specific hypotheses.

✔ **Principle 3: The hypothesis or hypotheses should be placed before the section on methods.**

The method section describes how the researcher tested the hypothesis. Therefore, the hypothesis should be stated before describing the methods used.

In journal articles, hypotheses are usually stated in the paragraph immediately preceding the major heading of "method." In theses and dissertations, the placement is approximately the same, although there may be some variation depending on the style manual in use at a particular institution.

✔ **Principle 4: It is permissible to use terms other than the term "hypothesis" to refer to a hypothesis.** The context and placement of the statement just before the method section usually make it clear that a hypothesis is being stated.

> **Example 4-A:** "On the basis of the above review, it was assumed that when teachers are provided only with the information about students' ethnic origin and sex, the teachers' judgments would be based on their stereotypic impression of the corresponding ethnic groups and sexes" (Guttmann and Bar-Tal, 1982, p. 519).

In Example 4-A, the authors describe their "assumption," which is clearly a hypothesis in the context of their research article.

> **Example 4-B:** "On the basis of the above evidence, it was speculated that gaze and touch (on the arm), along with the appropriate selection of interviewer sex . . ., would lead to greater compliance with a request to participate in a shopping mall interview concerning questions on advertising and television viewing behavior" (Hornik and Ellis, 1988, p. 540).

In Example 4-B, the authors' speculation is a hypothesis.

Although it is acceptable to use terms such as "assumption," "speculation," and "prediction" to refer to hypotheses in journal articles, the term "hypothesis" usually should be used in term projects, theses, and dissertations.

✔ **Principle 5: The degree of specificity required in a hypothesis depends on the context in which the hypothesis is presented.**

> **Example 5-A Without Context:** "It was expected that positive family environment characteristics would be related to higher levels of certainty in decision making and lower levels of negative affect."

The hypothesis presented in Example 5-A is quite vague without the context that immediately precedes it in the journal article.

Example 5-A With Context: "Findings regarding the relationships among the variables of family environment, decisions made by pregnant adolescents, the certainty with which these decisions are made, and the emotional reactions of these women have been inconsistent. The present study represents an effort to systematically explore these relationships. It was expected that positive family environment characteristics would be related to higher levels of certainty in decision making and lower levels of negative affect" (Warren and Johnson, 1989, p. 509).

The context for Example 5-A makes it clear that the hypothesis relates to decisions being made by pregnant adolescents.

Example 5-B Without Context: "It was predicted that a group of performance-anxious musicians receiving this multi-faceted treatment would show greater reduction in anxiety, related to musical performance, than a wait-list control group."

Example 5-B is a hypothesis because a hypothesis "predicts" the outcome of a study.

Example 5-B With Context: "The purpose of this pilot study is to evaluate the effectiveness of a treatment approach to musical performance anxiety, which combines the use of progressive muscle relaxation, cognitive therapy and temperature biofeedback training in the treatment of performance anxiety. It was predicted that a group of performance-anxious musicians receiving this multi-faceted treatment would show greater reduction in anxiety, related to musical performance, than a wait-list control group" (Nagel, Himle, and Papsdorf, 1989, p. 13).

When the hypothesis is considered in light of the purpose that provides the context in Example 5-B, the type of treatment to be tested is clear.

14

✔ **Principle 6: A hypothesis may be stated without indicating the type of relationship expected between variables. To qualify as a hypothesis, however, it must specify that some unknown type of relationship is expected.** Such a hypothesis is known as a "nondirectional" hypothesis because it does not specify the direction of the relationship. Example 6-A illustrates such a hypothesis for a descriptive study and Example 6-B illustrates it for an experimental study.

> **Example 6-A:** Low SES and high SES subjects differ in their levels of authoritarianism.

> **Example 6-B:** Adult males with condition X who are administered Drug A will report a different level of pain than a comparable group of adult males who receive Drug B.

Nondirectional hypotheses are less frequently used in research than directional hypotheses. This is probably true for two reasons: (1) researchers often have opinions about the variables they study, and their opinions often lead them to formulate directional hypotheses and (2) when researchers do not wish to speculate on the direction of a relationship, they may substitute a statement of the research purpose or research question for a hypothesis. This type of substitution is discussed in detail in Chapter 3.

✔ **Principle 7: When a researcher has a research hypothesis, it should be stated in the research paper; the null hypothesis does not always need to be stated.**

A research hypothesis is the hypothesis that the researcher believes will be supported by his or her data. For most research hypotheses, there are no direct statistical tests of the significance of the differences or relationships postulated. Rather, significance tests are designed to test null hypotheses, which state that there is no true relationship or difference in the population from which the samples were drawn.

Whenever a significance test is conducted, it is understood by the sophisticated reader that a null hypothesis is being tested. Thus, in most academic journals, formal statements of null hypotheses are omitted.

In term projects, theses, and dissertations, students are often required to state the null hypothesis in order to demonstrate that they understand what is being tested statistically. Examples 7-A and 7-B illustrate some ways in which the null hypothesis can be stated. Because there is more than one way to state a null hypothesis, two statements of the null hypothesis are shown in each example. Only one statement, of course, would be included in a research paper.

> Example 7-A: RESEARCH HYPOTHESIS: Private school graduates have a higher proportion of fathers in high status occupations than public school graduates.
>
> CORRESPONDING NULL HYPOTHESIS: There is no difference in the proportion of fathers in high status occupations between the populations of private school and public school graduates.
>
> ANOTHER VERSION OF THE NULL HYPOTHESIS: The observed differences between the proportions of fathers in high status occupations for private school graduates and public school graduates are the result of chance variations associated with the random sampling process.
>
> Example 7-B: RESEARCH HYPOTHESIS: Social standing in campus organizations is directly related to gregariousness.
>
> CORRESPONDING NULL HYPOTHESIS: There is no true relationship between social standing in campus organizations and gregariousness.
>
> ANOTHER VERSION OF THE NULL HYPOTHESIS: The relationship between social standing in campus organizations and gregariousness is nonexistent in the population from which the sample was drawn.

✔ **Principle 8: Avoid using the word "significant" in the statement of the null hypothesis.**

The word "significant" refers to a test of statistical significance that will be used to determine whether a null hypothesis should or should not be rejected. Because all null hypotheses should be tested with tests of significance, it is superfluous to incorporate a reference to significance testing into a statement of the null hypothesis.

In the Improved Version of Example 8-A, the word "true" has been substituted for the word "significant." A statistician defines a "true difference" as the difference that would be found if the variables could be studied without the presence of sampling errors (i.e., chance or random errors).

> **Example 8-A:** There is no significant difference in amount of recall of basic principles between students who read a 500-word passage on space travel and students who read a 100-word summary of the same passage.

> **Improved Version of Example 8-A:** There is no true difference in amount of recall of basic principles between students who read a 500-word passage on space travel and students who read a 100-word summary of the same passage.

EXERCISE FOR CHAPTER 2

In this exercise, you are asked to examine examples of published research in journals as well as theses and dissertations. There is no better way to learn the conventions followed in writing reports of empirical research than extensive reading of such reports.

1. Review journal articles and locate a statement that contains two or more hypotheses incorporated into a single sentence. Copy the statement and bring it to class for discussion.

2. Review journal articles and locate a statement that consists of a numbered list of three or more hypotheses. Copy the list and bring it to class for discussion.

3. Review four journal articles that contain explicit statements of hypotheses and make note of the following:
   a. In how many cases are the hypotheses stated in the last paragraph before the "method" sections?
   b. In how many cases are the hypotheses stated in the last sentence before the "method" sections?
   c. In how many cases did the authors use alternative terms such as "speculate" or "assume" rather than "hypothesize" in the statements of hypotheses?
   d. In how many cases would the statement of the hypothesis be vague if removed from the surrounding context? If any are judged to be vague without context, copy one of them and make notes on the context and how it helps illuminate the meaning of the hypothesis.
   e. How many of the hypotheses were directional and how many were nondirectional? If both types are found, copy an example of each.

4. Examine theses or dissertations in your college/university library. Copy a research hypothesis and the corresponding null hypothesis and bring it to class for discussion.

5. Write a set of related directional research hypotheses on a topic of interest to you. For each research hypothesis, write a corresponding null hypothesis.

6. Rewrite one of the hypotheses that you wrote for item number five to make it a nondirectional hypothesis.

Chapter 3

WRITING RESEARCH PURPOSES, OBJECTIVES, AND QUESTIONS

Often researchers do not state hypotheses either because they are not interested in examining relationships between variables or because they believe that there is too little knowledge on a topic to permit formulation of hypotheses. Under these circumstances, a research purpose or research question should be substituted for a hypothesis.[1] A research purpose is sometimes called a research objective.

The principles for writing hypotheses should be followed when writing research purposes and questions. The following principles indicate when to state the latter instead of hypotheses and illustrate the application of some of the principles in Chapters 1 and 2 when writing purposes and questions.

✔ **Principle 1: When the goal of research is to describe group(s) without describing relationships among variables, state a research purpose or question instead of a hypothesis.**

> **Example 1-A:** "Our research project was designed to collect empirical data on what the traditional graduate training programs in clinical psychology were doing to provide formal didactic and clinical training on the treatment of the suicidal patient" (Bongar and Harmatz, 1989, p. 210).

In Example 1-A, the authors state a research purpose; note that the authors do not use the term "purpose" in their statement. This example originally appeared immediately above the "method" section in the research article — the same position where hypotheses are usually

---

[1]Sometimes a hypothesis is preceded by a general statement of purpose; see "Example 5-B With Context" on page 14.

placed.

The authors of Example 1-A report responses to eleven questions such as "Does the clinical training program offer formal training (courses, seminars, etc.) in the study of suicide?" The responses to each question are reported separately and there is no attempt to relate one variable to another. Because a hypothesis indicates a relationship between variables, it would be inappropriate to formulate a hypothesis for this study.

Notice that the purpose in Example 1-A could have been stated as a research question, as illustrated in Example 1-B.

> **Example 1-B:** What are the traditional graduate training programs in clinical psychology doing to provide formal didactic and clinical training on the treatment of the suicidal patient?

The choice between stating a research purpose or a research question is a matter of choosing the form that reads more smoothly in a particular context. One form is not inherently preferable to the other.

✔ **Principle 2: When there is insufficient evidence to permit formulation of a hypothesis regarding a relationship between variables, state a research purpose or question.**

In a study of conflict in maritally distressed military couples, Griffin and Morgan (1988, p. 15) point out that most of the research in this area is dated; previous studies tend to emphasize the study of these variables under wartime conditions or focus on the stereotype of a military husband with a dependent homemaker wife. Furthermore, they point out that recent literature is contradictory on whether military couples have unique problems. Given this lack of current information on which to develop hypotheses, they formulated the research questions shown in Example 2-A.

> **Example 2-A:** "Specifically, the research question was: Are distressed military couples more likely to endorse certain items on the Areas of Change Questionnaire than their civilian

20

counterparts? And, does item endorsement vary as a function
of sex?"

In Example 2-A the authors are asking questions about
relationships. For example, the second part of the question asks
whether the way subjects respond is related to their sex. However, the
authors declined to hypothesize about the direction of the relationship
due to the lack of consistent, current information on the variables.

Example 2-A could be rewritten as a research purpose without
changing the meaning of the authors' statement, as illustrated in the
following example.

> **Example 2-B:** The purpose was to determine whether distressed
> military couples are more likely to endorse certain items on the
> Areas of Change Questionnaire than their civilian counterparts
> and to determine whether item endorsement varies as a
> function of sex.

✔ Principle 3: A research purpose or question should be as specific as possible, yet stated concisely.

The need for specificity in hypotheses is discussed in Chapters 1
and 2. Application of this principle to hypotheses, purposes, and
questions is often more difficult than one might realize at first.
Consider, for instance, Example 2-A shown above. It is quite specific,
actually naming a specific instrument (i.e., measuring tool). However,
for a reader who is not familiar with the Areas of Change Questionnaire, the research questions may be too specific. Thus, a writer must
judge whether his or her audience is likely to be familiar with the
specific item(s) mentioned—in this case, the specific questionnaire.

✔ Principle 4: When a number of related purposes or questions are to be stated, the author should consider presenting them in a numbered or lettered list.

Example 4-A: "The central questions asked in the study are: (a) Is the self-help treatment . . . better than no treatment at all? (b) Is the self-help treatment as effective as a similar therapist-led treatment? (c) What factors are associated with improvement when the self-help treatment is used?" (Morawetz, 1989, p. 366).

The lettered list in Example 4-A is easy for a reader to follow and allows the author to refer to individual hypotheses by letter later in the report.

Example 4-B: "Based on the field research and literature on job redesign, several questions guided the study:
1. What factors are important elements of teacher responses to the career ladder?
2. Do participants and nonparticipants differ in their attitudes about the career ladder?
3. Do teachers in various career stages differ in attitudes about the career ladder?
4. Does level of teaching (elementary, junior high, or senior high) influence teacher attitudes about the career ladder?
5. Do all teachers describe the reform as discomforting, or are changes evolving less disruptively?
6. How are authority and supervision relationships affected by the career ladder?" (Hart, 1987, p. 483).

Example 4-B is an example of a numbered list. Notice that the authors used a parenthetical expression to make the statement of the fourth question more specific.

Principle 4 is strongly recommended for beginning practitioners of empirical research writing. It is not always followed by experienced research writers, as illustrated in Example 4-C.

Example 4-C: "The present study was designed to add to existing knowledge regarding the interrelationships between self-esteem, gender, and dishonest behavior by focusing on a behavior that appears to be unambiguously more dishonest than behaviors studied to date, namely, actual cheating behavior in a classroom environment" (Ward, 1987, p. 710).

In Example 4-C, the author names three variables (i.e., self-esteem, gender, and dishonest behavior) among which relationships will be examined; he does not name each relationship separately. This is acceptable as long as the statement is clear and easy to follow, as it is in this case.

✔ **Principle 5: The adequacy of a purpose or question should be evaluated in light of the context in which it is stated.**

> **Example 5-A:** "The specific objectives of the study are (1) to determine the characteristics of the predators, the victim, and the target who does not become a victim; (2) to describe the setup process; and (3) to develop recommendations for the prevention of sexual assaults" (Chonco, 1989, p. 72).

In Example 5-A, it is not clear what type of sexual assaults are of interest to the author. The title (i.e., "Sexual Assaults Among Male Inmates: A Descriptive Study") and the introduction, which concludes with the statement of objectives shown above, make it clear that the study is on sexual assaults among male inmates.

EXERCISE FOR CHAPTER 3

1. Briefly describe the two conditions under which it would be better to state a research purpose or question rather than a research hypothesis.

2. In general, should the research question format be preferred over the research purpose format?

3. Review journal articles and locate a statement that consists of a

numbered list of purposes or questions. Copy the list and bring it to class for discussion.

4. Review four journal articles that contain explicit statements of purposes or questions and make note of the following:
    a. In how many cases are the purposes and questions presented in the last paragraph before the section on methods?
    b. In how many cases are the purposes and questions stated in the last sentence before the section on methods?
    c. In how many cases would the statement of the purpose or question be vague if removed from the surrounding context? If any are judged to be vague without context, copy one of them and make notes on the context and how it helps illuminate the meaning of the purpose or question.

5. Write a research purpose on a topic of interest to you. Then, rewrite it in order to make it into a research question. Which form (i.e., purpose or question) do you prefer? Why?

Chapter 4

WRITING TITLES

The following are principles for writing titles for empirical research reports.

✔ Principle 1: If only a small number of variables are studied, the title should name the variables.

In Example 1-A, the variables are self-esteem and aggressiveness.

Example 1-A: The Relationship Between Self-Esteem and Aggressiveness

Notice that the title in Example 1-A is not a complete sentence and does not end with a period mark, which are appropriate characteristics of titles.

✔ Principle 2: If many variables are studied, only the types of variables should be named.

For example, a researcher might examine how students' attitudes toward school change over time with attention to differences among urban, suburban, and rural groups; various socioeconomic groups; the sexes; and so on. Because there are too many variables to name in a concise title, only the central variable or variables need to be named and reference made to the other variables that were studied, as in Example 2-A.

Example 2-A: Changes in Students' Attitudes toward School and their Relationships with Selected Demographic Variables

25

✔ Principle 3: The title of a journal article should be concise; the title of a thesis or dissertation may be longer.

Titles of journal articles tend to be concise. A simple survey illustrates this point. A count of the number of words in the titles of a random sample of the 152 research articles on mathematics education that appeared in 42 journals during 1988 revealed that the median (average) number of words was about 11. Example 3-A is the shortest and Example 3-B is the longest.

Example 3-A: The Mathematics Department

Example 3-A is exceptionally short and could be improved by including reference to the types of variables studied.

Example 3-B: Grade Placement of Addition and Subtraction Topics in Japan, Mainland China, the Soviet Union, Taiwan, and the United States

Example 3-B is long only because the countries are listed. If it ended with "in Various Countries" it would be more concise but less descriptive.

Example 3-C: Contributions of Some Personality and Biographical Factors to Mathematical Creativity

Example 3-C shows a title of about average length for the sample of titles examined. It illustrates Principle 2; the *types* of variables, "personality factors" and "biographical factors," are named; the specific personality and biographical factors are not named.

A random sample of titles of dissertations on mathematics education during 1988 revealed that the median number of words in the titles was about 19, considerably more than the median of 11 for journal articles. The longest dissertation title in the sample is shown in Example 3-D.

Example 3-D: A Descriptive Study of Verbal Problems in Mathematics Textbooks, Grades Seven and Eight, from Five Time Periods: The Early-60s, the Early-70s, the Late-70s, the Early-80s, and the Late-80s

Although Example 3-D is quite long, it may be acceptable because the titles of dissertations and theses often are very specific and, therefore, long. Theses and dissertations are, in fact, tests; they permit students to demonstrate the breadth of their knowledge as well as their ability to write precise, detailed descriptions.

✔ **Principle 4: A title should indicate what was studied — not the results of the study.**

All of the previous examples illustrate this principle. Example 4-A violates the principle; it is corrected in the improved version.

Example 4-A: Girls Score Higher than Boys on All Tests Except Science

Improved Version of Example 4-A: Sex Differences on an Achievement Test Battery

Principle 4 may surprise some beginning students of empirical methods because outcomes and conclusions are often stated in titles in the popular press. This is the case because, quite often, the press reports straight-forward facts; "Five Die in Downtown Hotel Fire" is a perfectly acceptable title for a factual article of limited scope. Because research articles in academic journals are likely to raise as many questions as they resolve, a title that states a simple factual conclusion is usually inappropriate.

✔ **Principle 5: Mention the population(s) in a title when the type(s) of population(s) are important.**

Example 5: Teachers' Reactions to the Use of Calculators by Primary Level Students During Mathematics Examinations

By indicating that teachers' reactions are being reported, the authors indicate an important delimitation of the study.

✔ **Principle 6: Consider the use of subtitles to amplify the purposes or methods of study.**

In Examples 6-A and 6-B, the subtitles indicate the types or methods of study. In Example 6-C, the subtitle hints at a purpose of the study—to compare two types of counselors.

Example 6-A: Kindergarten Teachers' Definitions of Literacy: A Survey

Example 6-B: Literacy in the Kindergarten Classroom: A Case Study

Example 6-C: Counseling Patients with AIDS: Perspectives of Gay and Non-Gay Counselors

In Example 6-C, the type of client, patients with AIDS, is stressed by being placed near the beginning of the title. In Example 6-D, the emphasis is on the type of counselor. The choice between the two depends on the main thrust of the author's research.

Example 6-D: Perspectives of Gay and Non-Gay Counselors on Counseling Patients with AIDS

✔ **Principle 7: A title may be stated in the form of a question; this form should be used sparingly and with caution.**

Example 7-A: Are Interpretations of Thematic Apperceptive Test Protocols Influenced by Clinicians' Previous Knowledge of Client Behavior?

Example 7-A is cast in a form that implies that the answer will be a simple "yes" or "no," which is seldom the case in empirical research. This problem has been corrected below.

Improved Version of Example 7-A: To What Extent are Interpretations of Thematic Apperceptive Test Protocols Influenced by Clinicians' Previous Knowledge of Client Behavior?

Titles in the form of questions may suggest that straightforward answers will be found in the research article. Because this is often not the case in empirical research reports, such titles should be used with caution because they may be misleading.

Questions, when used as titles, have a less formal feel than titles in the form of statements. Thus, the question form sometimes may be preferred in less formal types of publications such as staff newsletters and in-service workshop materials.

✔ **Principle 8: Use the words "effect" and "influence" in titles with caution.**

The words "effect" and "influence" are frequently used in titles of research in which cause-and-effect relationships are examined. To examine such relationships, true experimental, quasi-experimental or rigorous ex-post facto methods should be employed; as a general rule, only the titles of reports employing these methods should contain these words.

Examples 8-A and 8-B illustrate the typical use of the word "effect" in a title; the general form is "The effect of an independent variable (treatments) on a dependent variable (outcomes)."

Example 8-A: The Effects of Three Schedules of Reinforcement on the Maze Performance of Rats

Example 8-B: The Effects of Handwriting Instruction on Legibility among Adult Learners

"Effect" is used as a noun in Examples 8-A and 8-B. As a noun, it means "influence." The word "affect," when used as a noun, means "feelings or emotions." Clearly, "effect" is the correct noun to use in these examples.

✔ **Principle 9: A title should be consistent with the research hypothesis, purpose, or question.**

In Example 9-A, a simple research purpose is stated; the corresponding title closely mirrors the statement of the purpose.

Example 9-A:

Research purpose: "The purpose of this study was to examine the relationship between mathematics performance and students' attitudes toward technology (computers and calculators), and to determine whether the relationship varied by gender" (Munger and Loyd, 1989, p. 169).

Corresponding Title of the Research Article: "Gender and Attitudes toward Computers and Calculators: Their Relationship to Math Performance"

In Example 9-B, three hypotheses are stated; the title refers to the major variables.

Example 9-B:

Research hypotheses: "(1) Stress will have more of a negative effect on the life satisfaction of the young/old (those elderly under age 75) than the old/old (those over age 75); (2) social support and activity will have more of a positive effect on the life satisfaction of the young/old than the old/old; (3) the buffering effect of social support will be stronger in the young/old than in the old/old" (Gray and Calsyn, 1989, p. 215).

Corresponding Title of the Research Article: "The Relationship of Stress and Social Support to Life Satisfaction: Age Effects"

In Example 9-B the authors state their expectations in the research hypotheses but, properly, not in the title.

EXERCISE FOR CHAPTER 4

PART A: Comment on the adequacy of each of the following titles for research articles.

1. Experimental Psychologists Have a More Positive Attitude Toward Statistics as a Tool for Understanding Human Behavior than Clinical Psychologists Have

2. The Clinical Psychologist

3. Adolescent Development

4. Adolescent Females React Favorably to Multicultural Novels

5. The Effects of Peer Coaching in Reading Among Fifth-Graders: An Experiment Conducted in Five Major Urban Areas During the 1992–1993 School Year Using Multiple Measures of Reading Comprehension with Analyses by Gender and Grade Level

6. Can Clinical Psychologists Prevent Suicide?

7. Criteria Used by Professors in the Selection of Statistics Textbooks

8. The Effects of Massive and Moderate Levels of Verbal Praise on the Out-of-Seat Behavior of Hyperactive Students

PART B: Select two of the hypotheses, purposes, or questions presented in Chapters 1, 2, or 3 and write an appropriate title for each.

PART C: Name a purpose for research on a topic of interest to you and write an appropriate title.

Chapter 5

WRITING INTRODUCTIONS
AND LITERATURE REVIEWS

The purpose of an introduction in an empirical research report is to introduce the problem area, establish its significance, and indicate the author's perspectives on the problem. Introductions usually conclude with an explicit statement of the research hypotheses, purposes, or questions to be answered by the study.

In a journal article, the introduction is almost always integrated with the literature review into a single essay. Most institutions of higher education require that the introduction and the review of literature in a thesis or dissertation be presented in separate chapters.

The principles that follow apply to all types of empirical research reports and proposals except where noted.

✔ **Principle 1: Start the introduction by describing the problem area; gradually shift its focus to specific research hypotheses, purposes, or questions.**

To implement Principle 1, first write a topic outline of what will be covered. Example 1-A shows a simple outline that illustrates Principle 1.

Example 1-A: Topic Outline for Introduction
1. Importance of question-asking by children
   a. As a functional skill in everyday life
   b. As a skill used in learning in school
2. Introduction to two types of questions
   a. Requests for factual information (Who, What, and When)
   b. Questions about causation (Why)
   c. Functions of the two types in school

3. Relationship between parents' verbal behavior and
   children's behavior
   a. On other verbal variables
   b. On question-asking behavior: quantity and type
4. Relationship between culture and verbal behavior
   a. Examples of how and why cultures may vary
   b. Functions of questions in target cultures
5. Statement of research purposes
   a. Determine types and numbers of questions asked
      in a structured learning environment
   b. Determine relationship between question-asking
      by parents and by children
   c. Determine relationship between question-asking
      and cultural background in target cultures

If the above outline were for an introduction in a thesis or
dissertation, the author would write the introduction with emphasis on
his or her own views and observations regarding these topics with few
citations to published literature; reference to the fact that certain topics
will be covered in more detail in the literature review, which is usually
the second chapter, would be appropriate.

If Example 1-A were an outline for an introduction to a journal
article, the literature review would be integrated with the author's
introductory remarks.

✔ **Principle 2: The significance of a topic should be explicitly stated in
the introduction to a term paper, thesis, or dissertation.**

Colleges and universities often require that the introduction to
a thesis or dissertation contain a subsection on the significance of the
research topic. Be specific in giving reasons for the importance of a
topic, as illustrated in Example 2-A.

Example 2-A: The need to investigate the training needs of
counselors who work with victims of AIDS at this time is
important because
   a. the number of cases of AIDS continues to increase,
creating greater demand for counselors trained in this area;

34

b. AIDS tends to occur more frequently in certain minority groups, which may have unique psychological needs; and

c. information on the disease and its treatment continues to emerge at a rapid rate, creating the need for on-going training of counselors.

Long, detailed statements of the significance of research topics are less common, although usually acceptable, in journal articles. Authors of articles often assume that their readers are specialists who already understand the importance of their topics and, thus, often provide less detailed descriptions of significance than are typically found in theses and dissertations. It is always a good idea, though, to indicate in the introduction why the original research being reported is significant to the field.

✔ **Principle 3: A statement of significance should be specific to the topic investigated.**

Example 3-A: Human resource is one of the greatest resources of this country, and education plays a major role in maintaining, nurturing and protecting that resource. It is imperative that we find, evaluate and utilize systems that yield the results that are necessary for the country's progress.

Example 3-A was submitted as the statement of significance in the first draft of the proposal for a thesis in which a functional skills program in adult schools was to be evaluated. Notice that the statement fails to deal specifically with functional skills in adult education. In fact, the statement is so broad, it could refer to almost any curriculum and instruction topic in education.

✔ **Principle 4: Use of the first person is acceptable; it should be used when it facilitates the smooth flow of the introduction.**

Use of the first person is especially appropriate when referring to the author's personal observations, experiences, and beliefs, as is the case in Example 4-A.

> **Example 4-A:** I began to speculate on the origins of this problem during my three years as an assistant to a teacher of the learning disabled.

The use of "I" to begin the sentence in Example 4-A is less stilted than the use of "This author."

Frequent use of the first person throughout the introduction and elsewhere in the research report, however, shifts the focus away from the content of the report, as in Example 4-B.

> **Example 4-B:** When I realized that all the previous research on this topic was descriptive, I decided that I would undertake an experimental study.

> **Improved Version of Example 4-B:** Because all the previous research on this topic was descriptive, an experimental study seemed to be in order.

✔ **Principle 5: The literature review should be presented in the form of an essay — not in the form of an annotated list.**

An annotation is a brief summary of contents; a list of annotations indicates what research is available on a topic but fails to organize the material for the reader because it does not indicate how the individual citations relate to each other and what trends the author has observed in the research.

An effective review of the literature is an essay organized around a topic outline (see Principle 1) and takes the reader from topic to topic. The literature on a topic is cited during the discussion of that topic. Articles with similar findings or methodologies may be cited together, as in Example 5-A, where four references are given for a common finding.

Example 5-A, as it appeared in Smylie (1988, p. 2): "Historically, the enhancement function of staff development has not been very successful. Guskey (1986) reports that virtually every major work on the subject in the last 30 years has emphasized its general lack of effectiveness. Indeed, as practiced in most school districts, staff development for the improvement of practice plays a small and ineffectual role in the professional lives of teachers (Hawley & Rosenholts, 1984; Howey & Vaughan, 1983; Joyce, Bush, & McKibbon, 1981)."

Note that in the Harvard method for citing references, only the authors' last names and year of publication are given. The names may be made part of the sentence, as in Example 5-B, or they may be included parenthetically at the end of the sentence, as in Example 5-C. In 5-B the emphasis is on the authorship; in 5-C the emphasis is on the content or idea being expressed. The choice among forms hinges on the emphasis you wish to make.

> **Example 5-B:** Doe (1992) reports that a major source of dissatisfaction among teachers appears to be the low social status accorded to their profession.

> **Example 5-C:** A major source of dissatisfaction among teachers appears to be the low social status accorded to their profession (Doe, 1992).

Also note that some style manuals suggest omitting quotation marks for long quotations, which should be set off in block style (i.e., indented more than the body of the text from both the right and left margins). Example 5-A is in block style, but because the block contains material that is not part of the quotation (i.e., Example 5-A as it appeared. . .), quotation marks were used. See the quotation on pages 97–98 in Appendix B for an example of block style without quotation marks.

✔Principle 6: The literature review should emphasize the findings of previous research — not just the methodologies and variables studied.

Example 6-A: Smith (1992) studied the social dynamics of this group in an intensive two-year case study.

Example 6-A violates the principle; in the improved version, the major finding is summarized.

Improved Version of Example 6-A: Smith (1992) found that respect for authority and leadership among this group declined significantly after the imposition of censorship. This study is important because, being based upon a two-year case study, it is the most intensive study to date of the effects of censorship on college students.

✔ Principle 7: Point out trends and themes in the literature.

After citing a number of studies, Kalichman and Craig (1991, p. 84) conclude their literature review with generalizations about the literature, as shown in Example 7-A.

Example 7-A: "Taken together, previous research indicates that clinicians are hesitant to report suspected abuse unless they are fairly certain that abuse is occurring. However, this conclusion is speculative, as previous studies have not presented cases in which abuse is likely to be occurring. In addition, previous research has been limited by including only a small number of noninteracting variables, and thus did not reflect the complexity of abusive situations. Finally, no study has investigated the relationship between psychologists' tendencies to report and previous reporting experiences."

✔ Principle 8: Point out gaps in the literature.

In Example 7-A and Example 8-A, gaps in the literature are noted.

Example 8-A: "Despite the psychological problems associated with binge eating and the likelihood that dyscontrol associated with binge eating deleteriously affects weight, to our knowledge no controlled treatment studies of this syndrome have been published. . . . Therefore, our study was intended to provide a preliminary investigation of the short-term efficacy of cognitive-behavioral treatment for binge eating. For this purpose a randomized, controlled trial of subjects assessed before and after treatment was conducted" (Telch, Agras, Rossiter, Wilfley, and Kenardy, 1990, pp. 629-630).

The authors of Example 8-A not only point out a gap but also indicate that their study is designed to fill the gap. This is an effective way to justify a study, which is discussed under the next principle.

✔ **Principle 9: Use the literature review to establish the need for the current study.**

Stodolsky, Salk, and Glaessner (1991, p. 93) conclude their integrated introduction and literature review with the paragraph shown in Example 9-A, which is used to justify their study.

Example 9-A: "Our research makes a distinctive contribution because it has a comparative subject matter focus. Much prior research on student motivation and perceptions of schooling has tended to ignore subject matter, assuming these qualities are rather general individual characteristics or apply to schooling in general. We agree with the suggestion of Licht and Dweck (1984) that student motivational characteristics may show different relationships to learning in different types of subject matters. The unique dimensions of learning in particular domains may not have received enough attention, even when prior investigators have situated their research in particular subject areas. The lack of data is especially evident when the goal is to understand the dimensions underlying students' thinking and attitudes about different school subjects."

✔ **Principle 10: The author should feel free to express opinions about the quality and importance of the research being cited.**

After citing a number of studies, the authors of Example 10-A applied Principle 10.

> **Example 10-A:** "As would be hoped, studies using comparable research strategies have generally yielded comparable estimates of the prevalence of nightmares and nightmare problems. However, all such studies have shared one methodological shortcoming: Invariably they have relied on retrospective self-reports for their information, typically asking subjects to estimate the number of nightmares they have had during the past year. The exclusive reliance on such reports is problematic because estimates regarding the frequency of an event can be biased by a variety of factors . . . ." (Wood and Bootzin, 1990, p. 64).

If no statement is made about the special strengths and weaknesses of previous research being cited, a reader is likely to assume that the author of the literature review believes that the research methodology was reasonably sound. Thus, it is not necessary to comment on the adequacy of all of the research cited.

✔ **Principle 11: The literature review for a journal article should be highly selective; the review for a thesis or dissertation may be less selective.**

The main criteria for selection should be relevance to the topic and the quality of research. Recency of publication usually should be a minor criterion in the selection of literature. In a thesis or dissertation, however, the student may wish to demonstrate his or her knowledge of recent literature by citing all of it regardless of quality, while pointing out major weaknesses. In a journal article, citations of research that is only peripheral to the topic or very methodologically weak may be omitted.

40

✔ **Principle 12: Peripheral research may be cited in a thesis or dissertation when no literature with a direct bearing on the research topic exists. The writer should call the reader's attention to the peripheral nature of the citations.**

For example, when Los Angeles first started implementing year-round school schedules, there was no research on this topic. There was research, however, on traditional school-year programs in which children attended school in shifts, on the effects of length of the school year, and on the effectiveness of summer school programs. Students who were writing theses and research papers on the Los Angeles program had to cite such literature in order to demonstrate their ability to conduct a search of the literature and to write a comprehensive, well-organized review of literature. Remember that a thesis or dissertation is, in part, a test of a student's ability to locate, collect, and integrate references.

In a journal article, it would probably suffice to say that a systematic search of the literature revealed no studies on this topic.

✔ **Principle 13: Use direct quotations sparingly in literature reviews.**

This principle holds for three reasons. First, direct quotations often do not convey their full meaning without context; quoting the context is usually less efficient than paraphrasing the main idea(s) of the author. Second, frequent quotations may disrupt the flow of the review because of the varying styles of the authors. Finally, quotations often bog the reader down in details that are not essential for the purpose of providing an overview of literature.

Direct quotations are appropriate when the writer of the review (1) wants to illustrate either the original author's skill at writing or lack thereof and (2) believes that the wording of a statement will have an emotional impact on the reader that would be lost in a paraphrase. These purposes seldom arise in presenting literature in an empirical research report.

✔ **Principle 14: Report sparingly the details of the literature being cited.**

Because the research being cited has already been published, the reader may obtain copies to learn the details.

Typically, reviews of literature in theses and dissertations contain more details on cited research than reviews of literature in journal articles. Even in theses and dissertations, however, the author should be selective in reporting details.

When commenting on the quality of research being cited (see Principle 10), brief reference should be made to those characteristics that make it strong or weak.

Concluding Comments

For many students, writing the introduction and review of literature is the most difficult part of writing an empirical research report. The principles presented above will only help you avoid some of the major pitfalls; they do not cover the other important matters in effective writing such as providing clear transitions and writing with a sparse but clear style. The latter can be mastered only through guided learning under the tutelage of an experienced writer and through extensive reading of effective prose.

If you lack confidence in your ability to write introductions and literature reviews, follow these rules:

1. Write a topic outline as illustrated under Principle 1 and take it with you when you consult with your instructor or committee. The outline will help them understand what you are trying to accomplish and make it easier for them to help you.

2. Read numerous reviews of literature, paying attention to how they are organized and how the authors make transitions from one topic to another.

3. After writing a first draft, first have it reviewed by friends and colleagues—even if they are not experts on your topic. Ask them to point out elements that are not clear. Effective introductions are

usually comprehensible to any intelligent lay person.

4. Be prepared to revise and rewrite. Because effective writing is achieved through this process, expect that your instructor, committee, or journal editor will request revisions.

EXERCISE FOR CHAPTER 5

1. Examine the introductions to four journal articles on a topic of interest to you and answer the following questions.

   a. How many are organized according to Principle 1? How many follow some other organizational pattern?

   b. In how many does the author explicitly state why the research topic is significant? If any, copy one statement and bring it to class for discussion.

   c. In how many does the author use the first person? If any, copy an example and bring it to class for discussion.

   d. In how many is the literature review integrated with the introduction?

   e. In how many does the author express opinions on the quality of at least some of the literature cited? If any, copy an example and bring it to class for discussion.

   f. In how many are one or more direct quotations included?

   g. To what extent are details of previous research cited?

2. Examine the introductions and reviews of literature in four theses or dissertations. Answer questions a through g in question 1.

3. Write a topic outline for an introduction to a research project of interest to you. Have it reviewed by two friends or colleagues and revise it in light of their comments. Bring to class both the first and second drafts for discussion.

Chapter 6

WRITING DEFINITIONS

Two types of definitions are usually found in empirical research reports. Conceptual definitions, which refer to the general concepts, are often presented in the introduction. Operational definitions, which define traits in concrete, step-by-step physical terms, are usually presented in the section on methods.

In theses and dissertations, conceptual definitions are often presented in a separate section of the introduction, with its own subheading. In journal articles, conceptual definitions are usually integrated into the introductory statement. Often, authors of journal articles assume that their readers are familiar with the general concepts and, thus, do not provide formal statements of conceptual definitions. In both types of reports, operational definitions should be provided in the section on methods.

This chapter presents principles on what to define and how to write conceptual and operational definitions.

✔ **Principle 1: All of the variables in a research hypothesis, purpose, or question should be defined.**

> **Example 1-A:** There is a direct relationship between newspaper reading habits and cultural literacy.

"Newspaper reading habits" and "cultural literacy" should be defined in the report on the hypothesis shown in Example 1-A.

✔ **Principle 2: A defining attribute of a population (also called a control variable) should be defined.**

> **Example 2-A:** There is a direct relationship between newspaper

reading habits and cultural literacy among adult education learners.

In Example 2-A, "adult education learners" is an attribute that should be defined.

✔ **Principle 3: Theories and models on which a thesis or dissertation are based should be formally defined. In a journal article, the author may choose to provide an informal definition and refer the reader to a publication in which it is described in detail.**

Example 3-A: In the introduction to a thesis, a student states, "The results will be discussed against the background of the deprivation model."

The "deprivation model" mentioned in Example 3-A should be defined.

✔ **Principle 4: Conceptual definitions should be specific.**

Example 4-A: Reading is defined as the process of deriving meaning from printed text.

The definition in Example 4-A is not sufficiently specific. In the improved version, information is given on the process.

Improved Version of Example 4-A: "Reading is defined as the recognition of written symbols which serve as stimuli to meanings built up through the reader's experience and brought up to the reader's consciousness" (Tinker, 1967).

The student who submitted the proposal containing the Improved Version of Example 4-A, chose to cite a definition previously offered by an expert. This is perfectly acceptable.

✔ **Principle 5: Operational definitions should be provided. As noted above, these are usually stated in the method section of a report or proposal.**

An operational definition is a definition in terms of physical steps. After reading an operational definition, the reader should be able to see in his or her mind's eye the physical operations that were used to measure a variable, to give treatments, to define a population, or to identify the relevant aspects of a model or theory.

> **Example 5-A:** Creative fluency was defined as the ability to produce many creative solutions to a problem within a standard time frame.

Example 5-A is not operational because one cannot picture the exact problem — what was and what was not judged as creative — and the length of the standard time frame. The improved version is more operational.

> **Improved Version of Example 5-A:** Creative fluency was defined as the number of uses a subject could name for a brick during one minute.

> **Example 5-B:** The stress-producing condition used for the experimental group was a mild verbal threat given by the experimenter.

Example 5-B is not operational because the reader does not know what specific physical things were done in the presence of the subjects. This has been corrected in the improved version.

> **Improved Version of Example 5-B:** In order to produce the stress-producing condition for the experimental group, the subjects were seated by an experimenter who was dressed in a white doctor's jacket. The experimenter introduced himself as a medical doctor who stated that for the purposes of the experiment, "You will receive a mild electric shock while we measure your blood pressure."

47

✔ **Principle 6: If a published instrument was used, the variable measured by that instrument may be operationally defined by citing the reference for it.**

> **Example 6-A:** In this study, verbal intelligence is defined as performance on the Verbal Scale of the Wechsler Adult Intelligence Scale: Revised (Wechsler, 1981).

Because most published tests cannot be reproduced legally and because many are too long to reproduce in a research report, reference to a test, as in Example 6-A, is sometimes the only way to provide an operational definition.

The Wechsler Adult Intelligence Scale: Revised is a popular test of intelligence, and most readers interested in this topic are likely to be familiar with it. For published tests that are not well known, writers should provide an overview of their physical characteristics (e.g., types of items, number of items, and time limits) and their statistical properties, especially reliability and validity data.

✔ **Principle 7: If an unpublished instrument was used, the whole instrument should be reproduced in the report or a source for a copy of the instrument should be provided in order to define operationally the variable that was measured.**

If a very short instrument, such as a short questionnaire, is used, a copy may be included in the body of the report. Longer instruments should be included in an appendix in a thesis or dissertation. Authors of journal articles should be prepared to supply copies of longer unpublished instruments to readers who request them. Providing sample test items, when this will not violate test security, is a good way to increase the operationalization of the variable measured with longer instruments.

✔ **Principle 8: Operational definitions should be sufficiently specific so that another investigator can replicate a study with confidence that he or she is examining the same variables under the same circumstances.**

A replication is an attempt to reproduce the results of a study by using the same methods. Replicability is the major criterion for judging the reliability of the results of empirical research. Inability to replicate results casts serious doubts on the validity of earlier studies.

Even definitions that appear to be highly operational at first glance may be inadequate when one attempts to replicate a study. The definition in Example 8-A illustrates this point. As one prepares to replicate a study involving this variable, questions about the physical process quickly arise: How large were the letters? What type of equipment was used to flash the letters? What type of screen was used? What type of film was used to produce the letters? and so on. Answers to these questions could easily affect the subjects' ability to recognize letters of the alphabet.

> **Example 8-A:** Visual acuity was defined as the ability to name letters of the alphabet when flashed on a screen in a random order for a period of two seconds for each letter.

Principle 8 is often not followed to the letter. In practice, the writer must consider how operational a definition needs to be in order to permit a reasonably close replication. For making fine discriminations among very similar shapes, answers to the questions posed about Example 8-A may be crucial to a successful replication.

✔ **Principle 9: Even a highly operational definition may not be a useful definition.**

An operational definition that is too narrow or is too far afield from how others define a variable may be inadequate. Example 9-A illustrates this point. It is fairly operational, but the definition of "self-concept" is much more narrow than that used by most psychologists and teachers.

> **Example 9-A:** Self-concept was defined as the number of times each child smiled during the first 15 minutes of homeroom for five consecutive days. A smile was defined as a noticeable upward turn where the lips meet — based on agreement by three independent observers. Each observer was a graduate student in clinical psychology. Counts of smiles were made from videotapes, which permitted the observers to reexamine facial expressions that were questionable.

Concluding Comments

Writing satisfactory operational definitions is often much more difficult than it might appear at first. When writing them, assume that you are telling someone exactly how to conduct your study. Then have your definitions reviewed by colleagues and ask them if they could perform the same study in the same way without requesting additional information. Use their comments in revising your definitions.

EXERCISE FOR CHAPTER 6

PART A: For each of the following definitions, describe what additional types of information are needed, if any, to make it more operational.

1. Math-anxiety was defined as manifest signs of anxiety during math-related activities.

2. Reading ability was defined as the Full Scale score on the Woodcock Reading Mastery Tests-Revised (Woodcock, 1987).

3. Language skills were defined as scores on a scale from one to ten

on essay tests in which students were asked to write three essays in a 50-minute period.

4. Hispanic students were defined as those students whose surnames appeared on a master list of Hispanic surnames developed by the author in consultation with two linguistic experts. This list may be obtained by writing to the author at P.O. Box xxx, Any City, State, Zip Code.

5. In this study, stress was defined as the condition that resulted from telling students that their success on a task that they were about to undertake would be used to make decisions about their placement in college.

PART B: Examine three research articles in journals and note how the variables in the research hypotheses, purposes or questions are defined. Copy the definition that you think is most operational and bring it to class for discussion.

PART C: Follow the directions for Part B but examine three theses or dissertations.

PART D: For each of the following variables, write a highly operational definition. Because you may not have studied some of these variables, do not concern yourself with whether your definitions are highly useful (See Principle 9).

6. ability to form friendships

7. math achievement

8. attitudes toward public institutions

9. respect for authority

10. an innovative method for teaching general psychology

PART E: Name a variable that you might wish to study. Write a conceptual definition of it and then write a highly operational definition. Try to make your operational definition both very operational and very useful (see Principles 8 and 9). For this activity, do not cite a published test or scale in order to define the variable you have selected. Have the definitions reviewed by colleagues and revise them. Bring both drafts of the two definitions to class for discussion.

Chapter 7

WRITING ASSUMPTIONS AND LIMITATIONS

An assumption is something that is taken to be true even though the direct evidence of its truth is either absent or very limited.

A limitation is either (1) a weakness or handicap that potentially limits the validity of the results or (2) a boundary to which the study was knowingly confined. The latter is often called a "delimitation." For example, if a researcher wanted to study artistic creativity in general but used only a measure of creative drawing, this would be a limitation in the first sense because it is a weakness in the execution of the study; if the researcher only wanted to study creative drawing and deliberately chose a measure of only this aspect of creativity, his or her findings would be delimited to this type of creativity, which is not a flaw in light of the investigator's purpose.

Explicit statements of assumptions, limitations, and delimitations are usually required in theses and dissertations. These statements are usually included in Chapter 1, each with its own subheading.

Authors of journal articles often integrate these statements in various sections of their articles, including the introduction, method section, and discussion section. They often are very selective in deciding which assumptions and limitations to state, naming only the major ones.

✔ **Principle 1: In the statement of an assumption, consider stating the reason(s) why it was necessary to make the assumption.**

In Example 1-A, Principle 1 has been violated because it states what was assumed but not why the assumption was necessary. Because no measure of human behavior is perfectly valid, Example 1-A adds little to the report. In the improved version, the author describes the circumstances that led to the use of a scale that may be of limited validity.

53

Example 1-A: It was assumed that the cheerfulness scale was valid.

Improved Version of Example 1-A: Because it was not possible to make direct observations and ratings of cheerfulness over time in a variety of settings, a self-report measure of cheerfulness was administered. Therefore, it was necessary to assume that the subjects were honest in reporting their typical levels of cheerfulness.

✔ **Principle 2: If there is a reason for believing an assumption is true, state the reason.**

Example 2-A: To encourage honest responses, the questionnaires were administered anonymously and the subjects were encouraged to be open and honest by the assistant who administered the scale.

If the sentence in Example 2-A were added to the Improved Version of Example 1-A, a partial basis for making the assumption would be indicated.

Example 2-B: Because the investigator could not be present in all of the classrooms while the experimental method was being used, it was necessary to assume that the teachers consistently and conscientiously used the method. This assumption seems tenable because the teachers were given intensive training, as described in the procedures section, and reported enthusiasm for the method, as described in the results section.

The last sentence in Example 2-B describes the basis for an assumption.

✔ **Principle 3: If an assumption is highly questionable, consider casting it as a limitation.**

Example 3-A: A certain number of the potential subjects refused to participate (15 of the 38 contacted by the male interviewer) . . . . It was assumed that the nonrespondents were similar to the respondents in their rate of weight reduction failures.

If the author has no basis for making the assumption in Example 3-A, the circumstance should be treated as a limitation — as was done in the Improved Version of Example 3-A.

Improved Version of Example 3-A, as it actually appeared in Reider (1987, pp. 35-36): "A certain number of the potential subjects refused to participate (15 of the 38 contacted by the male interviewer), either not responding on the telephone, or refusing to come in for an interview. Therefore, the sample actually studied necessarily excluded the uncooperative participants. It might reasonably be guessed that the subjects who refused to participate would have distorted their reports even more than those who cooperated because they likely contained a higher proportion of weight reduction failures."

The author of the Improved Version of Example 3-A refers to the circumstance as a "methodological problem," indicating that it is a limitation in the first sense described at the beginning of this chapter.

✔ **Principle 4: Consider speculating on the possible effects of a limitation on the results of the study.**

Reider (1987) followed this principle in the last sentence of the Improved Version of Example 3-A above. The last sentence in Example 4-A also illustrates this principle.

Example 4-A: "One possible limitation of the current findings is the measure of self-perceived problem-solving ability employed in the present study. The PSI is a general measure of problem-solving ability, and therefore, is not specific to the

55

experience of academic problems. The current results may have been even stronger if a measure that was tailored more specifically to the experience of academic problems had been used." (Blankstein, Flett, and Batten, 1989, p. 538).

✔ **Principle 5: When space permits, be specific in a statement of limitations.**

> **Example 5-A:** The population used in the study was restricted to students enrolled in a state college in a small town. Therefore, the findings of the study may not apply to other samples.

In Example 5-A, the writer fails to provide particulars; the improved version gives the reader a better feel for the extent of the limitation.

> **Improved Version of Example 5-A,** as it actually appeared in Motlagh (1968, p. 4): "The population used in the study was composed of sophomores, juniors and seniors enrolled at Fredonia State College, located in a small town of approximately 8,000 people. The students were primarily education and music majors. Therefore, the findings of the study may not apply to other samples."

✔ **Principle 6: Consider describing the two types of limitations (i.e., "weaknesses" and "boundaries," discussed at the beginning of this chapter) in separate sections or paragraphs. Refer to the first one as "limitations" and the second one "delimitations."**

> **Example 6-A:** "By design, the study is limited to law schools and doctoral programs in clinical psychology approved by the ABA and the APA . . . . Thus, it does not incorporate the many fine educational institutions which may have forensic psychology programs or an interest in preparing students to deal with

psycholegal issues, but are outside the ABA's and APA's stamp of approval" (Weber, 1986, pp. 18–19).

Example 6-A states a boundary to which the study was limited — it is not a weakness but rather a delimitation that the researcher put on the study. This statement could be included in a statement of the delimitations.

As indicated earlier, separate sections on limitations and delimitations with their own subheadings are more common in theses and dissertations than in journal articles.

EXERCISE FOR CHAPTER 7

1. Examine three theses or dissertations that contain explicit statements of assumptions. (The section on assumptions, if any, will usually be listed in the table of contents.) How many assumptions were written in accordance with both Principles 1 and 2? If any, copy one and bring it to class for discussion. If none, copy an assumption and name the principle(s) that were not followed.

2. How many of the individual assumptions that you examined for question 1 involved generalizing from a sample to a population? How many involved the measuring tools or tests? How many involved the administration of experimental treatments? How many involved other issues? Name them.

3. Examine three theses or dissertations that contain explicit statements of limitations. In how many did the authors speculate on the possible effects of the limitations on the results of their studies? (Note: This type of speculation may appear in the final chapter.) If any, copy an example and bring it to class for discussion.

4. How many of the individual limitations that you examined for question 3 involved generalizing from a sample to a population?

How many involved the measuring tools or tests? How many involved the administration of experimental treatments? How many involved some other issue?

5. How many of the individual limitations in the theses and dissertations that you examined for question 3 describe weaknesses and how many describe boundaries to which the study was deliberately confined? If both types are included, copy an example of each.

6. Suppose you mailed a questionnaire to each member of a population but only 28% completed the questionnaires and returned them to you. Suppose that you have no information on how the nonrespondents differ from the respondents. Would you describe this circumstance as an assumption or as a limitation? Why?

7. Suppose you used a standardized test that had been validated for the type of population that you were studying. Suppose that the test had high validity, but as with all tests, was somewhat less than perfectly valid. Would you describe this circumstance as an assumption or as a limitation? Why?

8. Suppose you administered both the experimental and control conditions to some experimental animals. You took extreme care to be sure that all animals were treated in the same way (diet, temperature, cage size, etc.) except for the administration of the treatments. Nevertheless, you realize that there is always the potential for human error no matter how careful a researcher tries to be. Would you state this circumstance as an assumption, as a limitation, or simply not refer to it in your paper? Why?

9. Consider a research project that you might wish to undertake. If you know of an assumption that you would probably need to make, write a statement describing it.

10. Consider a research project that you might wish to undertake. If you know of a limitation that you would probably have if you

conducted the study, write a statement describing it. For the same study, describe a boundary to which the study would probably be delimited.

NOTES

Chapter 8

WRITING METHOD SECTIONS

The section on methods contains a description of the physical steps taken to gather the data. Typically, it begins with a description of the subjects and instrumentation (i.e., measuring tools). Any additional procedures such as administration of experimental treatments should also be described here. Usually, it is better to overdescribe than underdescribe the methods employed, especially in the first draft of a report.

In reports on completed research, use the past tense to describe methods; in proposals, use the future tense.

✔ **Principle 1: The subjects should be described in enough detail so that the reader can visualize the subjects.**

> **Example 1-A:** "The children participating in this study were in the second grade at Leal Elementary School in the ABC Unified School District, Cerritos, California. The cultural make-up consisted of American students of the following ancestry or ethnic background: Japanese, Chinese, Filipino, Korean, Black, Mexican and varying degrees of European ancestry. The socio-economic level was middle to upper class. There were 22 students in the study, twelve boys and ten girls. Each group had six boys and five girls. The three special education students in the class were not included in the study" (Lopez, 1986, p. 18).

In Example 1-A, the reader can visualize the children's grade level, ethnicity, socioeconomic status, gender, and special education status.

When all the subjects are enrolled in a school or other institution, it is sometimes possible to obtain additional information from institutional records, such as achievement test scores, which could be summarized in order to describe the subjects more fully.

✔ Principle 2: When the sample is very small, consider providing a description of individual subjects.

After summarizing in general terms the ages and psychiatric histories of the ten subjects in their study, the authors of Example 2-A prepared a table that provides information on each individual (Schoenholtz, Horowitz and Shtarkshall, 1989, p. 101). Example 2-A shows a portion of that table.

Example 2-A: Portion of a table describing individual subjects.

Student	Age	Sex	Psychiatric Diagnosis
1	15	M	Major depression
			Attention deficit disorder
			Learning disability
2	18	M	Dysthymic disorder
			Conduct disorder
			Learning disability
etc.			

The complete table was about one-half of a page and provided detailed information on this unique group of subjects.

✔ Principle 3: A population should be named and the method used to select the sample should be described.

Example 3-A illustrates Principle 3.

Example 3-A: "Sixty subjects were randomly selected from the first grade population of Mexican-American children in a public school serving an economically disadvantaged area in Tucson, Arizona. Thirty of these subjects . . . ." (Henderson and Garcia, 1973, p. 195).

When samples of convenience are used, authors of journal articles often decline to explicitly state so in violation of Principle 3. If the method of selection is not stated, sophisticated readers assume that a sample of convenience was used.

✔ Principle 4: If there was attrition, state the number of subjects who dropped out, the reasons for the attrition, if known, and information about the drop-outs, if available.

Example 4-A illustrates this principle.

Example 4-A: Five of the subjects (two boys and three girls) dropped out of the study because their families moved out of the school district. All five were Hispanic and spoke English as a second language.

✔ Principle 5: If an unpublished instrument was used, describe it in detail.

Example 5-A: Attitude toward school was measured with a nine-item questionnaire developed for use in this study.

Example 5-A lacks sufficient detail.

Improved Version of Example 5-A: Attitude toward school was measured with a questionnaire developed for use in this study. It contained nine statements. The first three concerned attitudes toward academic subjects; the next three concerned attitudes toward teachers, counselors, and administrators; the last three concerned the social environment in the school. Subjects were asked to rate each statement on a five point scale from 1 (strongly disagree) to 5 (strongly agree).

Because the questionnaire in Example 5-A contains only nine items, the author should consider including all of the items in the body of the report. Longer instruments should be described in the methods section and included in appendices in theses and dissertations. If the instrument is included in an appendix, be sure to mention this fact in the methods section.

✔ **Principle 6: If a published instrument was used, briefly describe the traits that it was designed to measure, its format, and the possible range of score values.**

In Example 6-A, Coleman (1984, p. 215) followed this principle.

Example 6-A: "Those children whose parents volunteered to participate were administered the Piers-Harris Self-Concept Scale (The Way I Feel About Myself, Piers, 1969; Piers & Harris, 1964). The scale was group-administered within each classroom. The scale consists of 80 declarative statements, to each of which the respondents indicate whether the item describes the way they feel about themselves. Approximately half the items are worded positively and half negatively to reduce the possibility of social desirability and acquiescent response bias. Items were constructed at the third-grade reading level, but the scale can be used at lower reading levels when the administrator reads the items individually (Robinson & Shaver, 1976). Scores range from 0 to 80 on the total self-concept index."

Note that the author provided references that contain additional information on the test.

✔ **Principle 7: In theses and dissertations, information on reliability and validity should be summarized; in journal articles, it is usually sufficient to refer to a published source of information on these topics if the instrument is well-known and in widespread use.** The latter was done by Cornell (1989, p. 60) in Example 7-A.

Example 7-A: "The Revised Children's Manifest Anxiety Scale (RCMAS) is a 37-item yes/no questionnaire that provides an overall measure of chronic anxiety levels (Reynolds and Richmond, 1978). Information on test reliability and validity is contained in the RCMAS manual (Reynolds and Richmond, 1985)."

✔ **Principle 8: Experimental procedures, equipment, and other mechanical matters should be described in sufficient detail so that the study can be replicated.**

Example 8-A, by Pena (1986, pp. 47-48), describes the treatment administered to one group in an experiment.

Example 8-A: "Each day the trade books used in the study were taken from their storage place and set on a large table. They were only used during the read-aloud sessions. All the children in this group would sit together to receive some instruction or modeling of how they were expected to read aloud. After the instruction the children would join their partners and together they would select the books to be read that day. It should be noted that at the end of the month, the trade books were taken back to the public library and exchanged for other animal and humor stories listed in the recommended reading handbook and 'Children's Choices' (Roth and Pitluk, 1985; International Reading Association, 1983, 1984)."

Some subjectivity enters into the decision as to how much detail to provide; in most cases, authors of published research do not provide every detail of the procedures. Instead, they try to provide enough to permit a reasonably close replication.

EXERCISE FOR CHAPTER 8

1. Locate a description of subjects that is highly detailed in a journal article, thesis, or dissertation. Bring it to class for discussion.

2. Locate a description of subjects that lacks sufficient detail. Copy it and briefly describe other types of information that might have been included to give a better picture of the subjects.

3. Examine the description of subjects in five sources. In how many did the authors provide descriptions of individual subjects? In how many did the authors explicitly name a population? In how many did the authors state that random selection from a population was used? In how many did the authors state that there was attrition and, if any, in how many were the reasons for the attrition given?

4. Examine the description of the instrumentation in the five sources that you used for question 3. In how many was an unpublished instrument used? If any, copy the description and indicate whether you believe that the description is sufficiently detailed.

5. Examine the description of procedures in the five sources that you used for question 3. Copy the one that is most detailed. Briefly describe whether you think it is sufficiently detailed and why.

Chapter 9

WRITING ANALYSIS AND RESULTS SECTIONS

The analysis and results section usually follows the section on methods. In a proposal, the proposed method of analysis should be described; the anticipated results may also be discussed.

✔ **Principle 1: Organize the analysis and results section around the research hypotheses (or purposes or questions) stated in the introduction; describe the analysis and results for the first hypothesis first, then describe them for the second hypothesis, and so on.**

If you presented a numbered list of hypotheses earlier in the report, refer to the content of each hypothesis and its number in order to identify it. Example 1-A illustrates this principle.

> **Example 1-A:** "Hypothesis 1 stated that professors' verbal responses to minority students' questions will be less complex than responses to non-minorities. Complexity was broadly defined in the following manner: *Direct Answer*: a brief, factual response with no additional explanatory comments (least complex); *Clarification Answer:* a factual but more explanatory answer to the students' questions (more complex); and *Elaboration*: an explanation done in an elaborative manner, generating more material than is necessary to answer the question (most complex).
>
> Hypothesis 1 was not supported. Professors showed no significant differences in *number* of Direct Answers, $F(1, 13) = .00, p > .05$; Clarification Answers, $F(1, 13) = .33, p > .05$; and Elaborations $F(1, 13) = .06, p > .05$. General statistics for Hypotheses 1–4 are reported in Table II.
>
> Hypothesis 2 stated that . . . ." (Trujillo, 1986, p. 635).

✔ **Principle 2: Standard statistical procedures need only be named; you do not need to show the formulas.**

Likewise, it is usually unnecessary to name the particular computer program used in the analysis.

✔ **Principle 3: Raw scores are usually not reported; only the statistics based on them are reported.**

The major exception to this principle is when only a very small number of subjects was studied. Also, in a thesis or dissertation, where space is not at a premium, raw scores may be given in an appendix, although this is not always required.

✔ **Principle 4: Present descriptive statistics first, usually starting with measures of central tendency and variability (or, for categorical data, starting with frequencies and percentages).**

For each set of scores, provide information on central tendency and variability (usually the means and standard deviations) before presenting correlation coefficients, if any, and the results of inferential tests. For example, correlation coefficients may provide direct information on the research hypotheses; even if this is the case, report measures of central tendency and variability first. These measures will show your reader what the average subject was like and how variable the group was.

For categorical data, present frequencies and percentages before presenting the results of inferential tests.

✔ **Principle 5: Organize large amounts of data in tables and give each table a number and a descriptive title (i.e., caption).**

Each title usually should name the statistics presented in the table and refer to the variables that were measured. The following examples illustrate this.

Example 5-A: Means and Standard Deviations for the Five Achievement Variables

Example 5-B: Number of Subjects Broken Down by Sex and Grade Level.

Example 5-C: Analysis of Variance for Verbal Fluency

Table numbers and titles usually are placed immediately above the tables. Titles do not need to be long to be effective, as illustrated in Example 5-D.

Example 5-D:

Table 1   Means and Standard Errors for Self-Report Ratings of Nausea by Bulimics and Controls

Nausea self-report measure	Controls		Bulimics	
	M	SE_M	M	SE_M
Nausea duration	1.3	0.1	3.1	0.6*
Nausea severity	0.3	0.1	2.0	0.6*

Note: For nausea duration, 1 = none, 7 = all the time. For nausea severity, 1 = very mild, 7 = very severe.
*$p < .01$.

Source: Broberg, D. J., Dorsa, D. M., & Bernstein, I. L. (1990, p. 185). Nausea in bulimic women in response to a palatable food. *Journal of Abnormal Psychology, 99,* 183–188. Copyright 1990 by the American Psychological Association. Reprinted by permission.

✔ **Principle 6: In the text, describe the main conclusions to be reached based on each table and point out highlights that the reader may otherwise overlook. You do not need to discuss each entry in a table.**

To describe all of the entries would be redundant. Broberg, Dorsa, and Bernstein (1990, p. 185) illustrate this principle when discussing the table shown in Example 5-D above. Their discussion is shown in Example 6-A; note that they describe the major trends in the table and present additional information on the t tests that they conducted.

> **Example 6-A:** "Nausea duration and nausea severity ratings are shown for each group in Table 1. Bulimics reported nausea to be of longer duration, $t(24) = 3.4$, $p < .01$, and of greater severity, $t(24) = 3.26$, $p < .01$, than did controls."

For a table containing 19 numerical entries, Hayes and Hambright (1984, p. 421) provided the description in Example 6-B.

> **Example 6-B:** "Data pertaining to the influence of socioeconomic position on the two moral typologies are presented in Table 2. The chi square value of .64 does not exceed the critical value level. Hence, socioeconomic status was not a significant factor in determining the type of moral judgments expressed by the subjects in this investigation."

For a table containing 25 numerical values, Kvet (1985, pp. 50-51) provided the description in Example 6-C.

> **Example 6-C:** "Table 3 presents the correlation matrices for all four districts. The values obtained show relationships ranging from moderate negative to moderate positive, both of which are in District A. However, a majority of the correlations range from weak positive to weak negative."

Note that the authors refer to the tables by number. Do not use phrases such as "The table below indicates." You cannot be certain of the placement of a table when your report is typed or typeset.

✔ Principle 7: Statistical figures (i.e., drawings such as histograms) should be professionally drawn and used sparingly in journal articles.

Figures may be used to organize and describe data; however, they usually take up more space than a corresponding statistical table would. Because space in journals is expensive, figures should be used sparingly. In theses and dissertations, where space is not limited, they may be used more frequently.

✔ Principle 8: Statistical symbols should be underlined or italicized.

> **Example 8-A:** The mean of the experimental group was significantly higher than the mean of the control group ($t = 2.310$, $df = 10$, $p < .05$, two tailed).

In Example 8-A, the statistical symbols are italicized. If you do not have the ability to italicize, underline the symbols; typesetters recognize underlining as a direction to italicize.

✔ Principle 9: Use the proper case for each statistical symbol.

Many letters in statistics have two meanings, which are differentiated by their case. For example, a lower-case f stands for "frequency"; an upper-case F is an inferential statistic used in significance testing.

✔ Principle 10: Numerals that start sentences and that are less than 10 usually should be spelled out.

The primary exceptions to this rule are when authors refer to elements in a numbered set such as "Chapter 1" or "Principle 2" or when presenting precise numerical results; for example, see Example 8-A.

✔ **Principle 11: Qualitative results need to be organized and the organization made clear to the reader.**

In qualitative studies, quantitative data often are not reported. Instead, the authors may report on major trends and themes that emerged from subjective analyses of data such as transcribed interviews. The discussion of such results should be organized; consider using subheadings to guide the reader in the discussion.

> **Example 11-A:** In discussing the qualitative results of a number of interviews with teachers who gathered in a bar each Friday after school, Pajak and Blase (1984) provided these subheadings: The Setting, The Job of Teaching, and The Meaning of the Setting. Direct quotations were used to illustrate the major findings.

> **Example 11-B:** In discussing the qualitative results of a study on the accommodations in a high school that encourage students to remain academically engaged, Miller, Leinhardt, and Zigmond (1988) used these subheadings to organize their results: Accommodation at the Institutional Level, Accommodation at the Classroom Level, Personal Accommodation, Accommodation in LD and Regular Education Settings, and Effects of Accommodation.

EXERCISE FOR CHAPTER 9

1. Examine the results sections of two published articles. Determine whether the authors followed Principle 4. Be prepared to discuss your findings in class.

2. Locate a statistical table in a published article that you think has a good title (i.e., caption). Make a photocopy of it and bring it to class for discussion. Be prepared to discuss whether the author followed Principle 5.

3. Locate a statistical figure in a published article and discuss whether presentation in the form of a table would have been as effective.

Chapter 10

WRITING DISCUSSION SECTIONS

The following are principles for writing the last section of the body of a journal article or the last chapter of a thesis or dissertation. Note that in brief journal articles, the results and discussion sections are often integrated into a single section.

✔ **Principle 1: A brief summary of the study may be included in the discussion section of a journal article; a longer, formal summary may be required in a thesis or dissertation.**

In a brief journal article, the author may omit a summary of purposes or methods. At the end of a long article, a summary is desirable.

✔ **Principle 2: If hypotheses were stated in the introduction, it is usually appropriate to restate them and indicate whether they were supported by the data.**

This principle is illustrated by Michalski and Guile (1990, p. 240), who began their discussion section with this paragraph:

Example 2-A: "The hypothesis that simplification of the language of state questions would decrease the likelihood of passage in a simulated voting experiment was supported. The subjects reading the simplified state questions were significantly more likely to vote negatively than were the subjects reading equivalent but less readable questions."

✔ Principle 3: Highlights of the results should be described in the discussion section.

This principle is illustrated in Example 2-A above and by Ware and Lee (1988, p. 604), who began their discussion section with the material in Example 3-A.

Example 3-A: "The results of this study provide additional evidence of women's continuing underrepresentation in science at the college level. In fact, the percentage of women students reporting the choice of a science major in this nationally representative sample of high-ability students (14%) is well below that reported by the National Science Foundation for 1983 graduates."

Spiegel, Wadden, and Foster (1991, p. 65) also began their discussion with a summary of results as well as a caution. The first paragraph of their discussion is shown in Example 3-B.

Example 3-B: "This study shows that subjects slow their rate of eating, as measured objectively, during behavioral treatment for obesity. A slower rate of eating was associated with greater weight loss at week 28. Thus, slowing the rate of eating appears to be of benefit. More evidence is needed, however, to demonstrate that there is a causal relationship between these two variables."

✔ Principle 4: When possible, explicitly state the implications of the results in the discussion section.

The implications of a study are usually cast in terms of actions that individuals should take based on the results of a study. Ward and Lee (1988, p. 607) provide a clear statement of the implications of one of their results, as shown in Example 4-A.

Example 4-A: "This study is especially significant for secondary level teachers and counselors, as it suggests that their advice can make a difference in the academic choices their female students make. An active interest on the part of teachers and counselors in girls' academic progress, manifested in the form of encouragement of able students to enroll in college preparatory courses and continue their educations after high school, does seem to influence women more than men to choose the science and mathematics courses that are crucial to their future scientific involvement. Knowing this, educators interested in promoting the scientific futures of promising female students might wish to initiate discussion with these students that would directly stress the importance of continuing to take science and mathematics in high school and college, while suggesting that they consider scientific majors and careers."

Stating the implications of a study at the end of the discussion section often provides a strong ending to an article. Example 4-B, shows the concluding paragraph by Karnes and D'Ilio (1989, p. 78).

Example 4-B: "These findings have implications for the development of leadership concepts and skills in the home and at school. Parents and teachers, through a variety of creative ideas and activities, need to expose their children to nontraditional roles and need to be made more aware of the increasing trend of women entering the work force in nontraditional leadership positions. Girls need continually to be reinforced and exposed to new roles and encouraged to participate in them."

If you have conducted a pilot study as a project for a research class, you may wish to hedge a bit in your statement of implications by beginning the statement with a caution as shown in Example 4-C.

Example 4-C: If the results obtained in this pilot study are confirmed in more definitive studies, the following implications should be considered by . . . .

✔ **Principle 5: Important strengths and limitations should be mentioned in the discussion section.**

Strengths and limitations of the research methodology should first be discussed in the section on methods. Important strengths and limitations that affect the interpretation of data should be mentioned again in the discussion section.

Clark (1991, p. 142) begins her discussion section by noting a weakness, which is shown in Example 5-A.

> **Example 5-A:** "The fact that the present study was based on such a small sample size makes it necessary to use caution in interpreting the results."

The authors of Example 5-B note both strengths and limitations in their discussion section.

> **Example 5-B:** "The design of the present study improved on previous methodologies by using random assignment, appropriate control groups for effects of assessment and the standard available intervention, and systematic outcome assessment including self-monitored drinking. The study is limited by the small sample size, the large variability in drinking measures, and the exclusive reliance on self-report to assess alcohol use. Although there was considerable consistency among the various types of self-report drinking measures, it would be preferable to have more thorough information on subjects' experience of adverse effects from alcohol use and independent corroboration from other sources such as friends, laboratory markers, or direct observations.
>
> Despite these limitations, the present findings are more encouraging than those of most previous studies. On the basis . . . ." (Kivlahan, Marlatt, Fromme, Coppel, and Williams, 1990, p. 809).

✔ **Principle 6: If you issue a call for further research on a problem, provide the reader with specific guidance.**

Few studies are conclusive; additional research on important problems is usually needed. Therefore, it is of little value to merely tell a reader that more research is recommended. The reasons why more research is needed and the form that it might take should be stated. This is illustrated in Example 6-A.

> **Example 6-A:** "This study, therefore, raises some questions and directions for future research in applications of computer therapy. Foremost among these questions is whether the weight-loss achieved with computer-assisted treatment can be brought to a level equal to that of the average short-term behavior therapy treatment, i.e., 5.0 k.g. In this study we achieved only half of this goal. Superior hand-held computers having more memory and greater ease of use are now available at the same cost of the computer used in this study. It is possible that with more memory available a more sophisticated interactive program might achieve better results. This question is eminently testable in the next phase of research" (Agras, Taylor, Feldman, Losch, and Burnett, 1990, p. 108).

✔ **Principle 7: Point out consistencies and inconsistencies of the current results with those in the literature cited earlier in the report.**

Application of this principle reminds the reader of the scientific context within which the study was conducted and helps the reader see how the current results contribute to the literature.

Principle 7 was applied by Arnett (1990, p. 178) in the following example.

> **Example 7-A:** "There was also a significant relation between sex without contraception and egocentrism, in that girls who had engaged in sex without contraception underestimated the probability of becoming pregnant as a result, compared to girls who had not. This cognitive distortion has been noted in a number of other studies (Gerrard et al., 1983; Goldsmith et al., 1972; Kalmuss, 1986; Oskampt and Mindick, 1981), but those studies were plagued by problems of sample selection and

77

representativeness in ways that the present study was not. The findings presented here make it possible to generalize to a wider population the notion that contraceptive nonuse among female adolescents is due partly to a tendency to distort the probability that pregnancy will result."

✔ **Principle 8: It is acceptable to speculate on the meaning of the results.**

When an author speculates, he or she is going beyond the data in order to show the reader some ways in which to think about the results. In the discussion section, authors should make it clear which statements are based on data and which are speculative in nature. The safest way to do this is to introduce speculative statements as such, which was done by Nuttall, Chieh, and Nuttall (1988, p. 193) in Example 8-A.

> **Example 8-A:** "Chinese children tended to include their parents and extended family members more often in their drawings than did U.S. children. One can speculate that they tended to see themselves as members of nuclear and extended families, whereas U.S. children expressed a greater sense of individualism and independence from their families."

✔ **Principle 9: It is usually inappropriate to introduce new data or new references to literature in the discussion and conclusion section.**

The final section of the body of the report should be used to summarize and interpret what was presented earlier. The introduction of new data or references distracts from this purpose.

EXERCISE ON CHAPTER 10

1. Locate a journal article in which the implications of the results are clearly stated in the discussion and conclusions section. Be prepared to discuss it in class.

2. Locate a journal article in which the author points out consistencies and inconsistencies with research he/she cited earlier in the article. Be prepared to discuss it in class.

3. Read a journal article but do not read the discussion and conclusion section. Write a discussion and conclusion section for it and then compare your material with that provided by the author(s) of the article.

NOTES

Chapter 11

WRITING ABSTRACTS

An abstract is a summary that is placed before the introduction in a journal article, thesis, or dissertation. Usually journals and universities put word limits on abstracts, often about 150 words.

✔ **Principle 1: Highlights of the results usually should be included in the abstract.**

Lee and Ekstrom (1987, p. 287) emphasize their results in their abstract, which is shown in Example 1-A.

Example 1-A: "The advice students receive on selecting a high school curriculum track or planning an appropriate course of study is likely to come from both home and school. The primary mechanism in America's public high schools to assist students in making informed decisions about these important choices is guidance counseling. Using data from the first and second follow-ups of *High School and Beyond,* including student self-reports, test scores and high school transcripts, we found that guidance counseling services appear to be unequally available to all public high school students. Students from families of lower socioeconomic status (SES), of minority status, and from small schools in rural areas are less likely to have access to guidance counseling for making these important decisions at the beginning of their high school careers. Moreover, students who lack access to guidance counseling are more likely to be placed in nonacademic curricular tracks and to take fewer academic math courses. It appears that students who may need such guidance the most, since they come from home environments where knowledge of the consequences of curricular choices is limited, are least likely to receive it in their schools."

✔ **Principle 2: Highlights of the methodology usually should be mentioned.**

Lee and Ekstrom refer to their methodology in the third sentence of Example 1-A. Farrell, Peguero, Lindsey, and White (1988) give more attention to the methodology in their abstract, which is shown in Example 2-A. Note that these authors used an innovative methodology, so more attention to it is appropriate in the abstract.

> **Example 2-A:** "The concerns of students identified as at-risk of dropping out of school in an urban setting were studied using innovative ethnographic methods. Students from the subject population were hired to act as collaborators rather than informants and to collect taped dialogues between themselves and their peers. As collaborators, they also participated in the analysis of data and contributed to identifying the research questions of the inquiry. Data indicated that pressure and boredom were most often mentioned as negative factors in the lives of the students, with pressure emanating from social forces outside of school but contributing to boredom inside."

✔ **Principle 3: Reference to the research purposes, questions, or hypotheses usually should be made.**

In Example 3-A, the authors begin their abstract with a statement of their hypothesis.

> **Example 3-A:** "The study tested the hypothesis that varying levels of parent involvement would be related to variations in qualities of school settings, specifically school socioeconomic status, teacher degree level, grade level, class size, teachers' sense of efficacy, principals' perceptions of teacher efficacy, organizational rigidity, and instructional coordination. Teachers . . . ." (Hoover-Dempsey, Bassler, and Brissie, 1987, p. 417).

In Example 3-B, the authors mention a general purpose, three hypotheses, and results relating to the hypotheses.

Example 3-B: "The purpose of this investigation was to develop and implement an instrument to analyze stories written by children to determine if sex-stereotyped roles were apparent in the main characters they created. The Analysis of Character Traits (ACT) was developed utilizing selected criteria identified in studies in which adults' stories for children were analyzed for sex stereotyping. Three research hypotheses were tested to determine if there was a significant relationship between the presence of stereotyping in main characters and the sex of the authors. The following conclusions were made: (1) male and female authors almost exclusively tended to create both stereotyped and non-stereotyped characters of their own sex; (2) sex stereotyping occurred in the characters created by both male and female authors to the same extent; and (3) differences in the profiles of male and female characters were present" (Tuck, Bayliss, and Bell, 1985, p. 248).

In Example 3-C, Schinke, Gordon, and Weston (1990, p. 432) state their purpose in the first sentence of their abstract, then briefly describe their methods, and, finally, describe the highlights of their results. This arrangement is recommended.

Example 3-C: "This study tested the efficacy of self-instruction intervention to reduce avoidable risks for HIV infection associated with drug use and unsafe sexual activity among African-American and Hispanic adolescents ($N = 60$). After completing pretests, adolescent participants in the study were randomly divided into three conditions. Participants in one condition received a self-instructional guide about AIDS and its transmission along with group instruction in using the guide. Adolescents in another condition received the guide without group instruction. Participants in the third condition received neither the guide nor group instruction. Outcome findings indicate that participants in the two self-instruction conditions improved more between pretest and posttest assessments on measures of HIV infection risk compared with adolescents in the control condition."

83

✔ **Principle 4: The abstract for a journal article usually should be a single paragraph.**

Students who are writing theses and dissertations should determine their institutions' requirements regarding length and number of paragraphs.

EXERCISE FOR CHAPTER 11

1. Locate an abstract for a journal article that you believe illustrates the four principles presented in this chapter. Photocopy it and be prepared to discuss it in class.

2. Locate a journal article of interest to you and read the article without reading the abstract. Write your own abstract for the article and compare it with the abstract prepared by the author of the article.

REFERENCES

Agras, W. S., Taylor, C. B., Feldman, D. E., Losch, M., & Burnett, K. F. (1990). Developing computer-assisted therapy for the treatment of obesity. *Behavior Therapy, 21,* 99–109.

Arnett, J. (1990). Contraceptive use, sensation seeking, and adolescent egocentrism. *Journal of Youth and Adolescence, 19,* 171–180.

Blankstein, K. R., Flett, G. L., & Batten, I. (1989). Test anxiety and problem-solving self-appraisals of college students. *Journal of Social Behavior and Personality, 4,* 531–540.

Bongar, B., & Harmatz, M. (1989). Graduate training in clinical psychology and the study of suicide. *Professional Psychology: Research and Practice, 20,* 209–213.

Chonco, N. R. (1989). Sexual assaults among male inmates: A descriptive study. *The Prison Journal, LXVIX,* 72–82.

Clark, J. Z. (1991). Therapist narcissism. *Professional Psychology: Research and Practice, 22,* 141–143.

Coleman, J. M. (1984). Mothers' predictions of the self-concept of their normal or learning disabled children. *Journal of Learning Disabilities, 17,* 214–217.

Cornell, D. G. (1989). Child adjustment and parent use of the term "gifted." *Gifted Child Quarterly, 33,* 59–64.

Farrell, E., Peguero, G., Lindsey, R., & White, R. (1988). Giving voice to high school students: Pressure and boredom, ya know what I'm sayin'? *American Educational Research Journal, 25,* 489–502.

Gray, D., & Calsyn, R. J. (1989). The relationship of stress and social support to life satisfaction: Age effects. *Journal of Community Psychology, 17,* 214–219.

Griffin, W. A., & Morgan, A. R. (1988). Conflict in maritally distressed military couples. *The American Journal of Family Therapy, 16,* 14–22.

Guttmann, J., & Bar-Tal, D. (1982). Stereotypic perceptions of teachers. *American Educational Research Journal, 19,* 519–528.

Hart, A. W. (1987). A career ladder's effect on teacher career and work attitudes. *American Educational Research Journal, 24,* 497–503.

Hayes, D. H., & Hambright, J. E. (1984). Moral judgment among black adolescents and white adolescents from different socioeconomic levels. *Journal of Negro Education, 53,* 418–423.

Henderson, R. W., & Garcia, A. B. (1973). The effects of a parent training program on the question-asking behavior of Mexican-American children. *American Educational Research Journal, 10,* 193–201.

Hoover-Dempsey, K. V., Bassler, O. C., & Brissie, J. S. (1987). Parent involvement: Contributions of teacher efficacy, school socio-economic status, and other school characteristics. *American Educational Research Journal, 24,* 417–435.

Hornik, J., & Ellis, S. (1988). Strategies to secure compliance for a mall intercept interview.

Public Opinion Quarterly, 52, 539–551.

Kalichman, S. C., & Craig, M. E. (1991). Professional psychologists' decisions to report suspected child abuse: Clinical and situation influences. *Professional Psychology: Research and Practice, 22,* 84–89.

Karnes, F. A., & D'Ilio, V. R. (1989). Leadership positions and sex role stereotyping among gifted children. *Gifted Child Quarterly, 33,* 76–78.

Kivlahan, D. R., Marlatt, G. A., Fromme, K., Coppel, D. B., & Williams, E. (1990). Secondary prevention with college drinkers: Evaluation of an alcohol skills training program. *Journal of Consulting and Clinical Psychology, 58,* 805–810.

Kvet, E. J. (1985). Excusing elementary school students from regular classroom activities for the study of instrumental music: The effect on sixth-grade reading, language, and mathematics achievement. *Journal of Research in Music Education, 32,* 45–54.

Lee, V. E., & Ekstrom, R. B. (1987). Student access to guidance counseling in high school. *American Educational Research Journal, 24,* 287–310.

Lopez, A. W. (1986). *Teaching punctuation in primary grades: A comparison of two strategies.* Unpublished master's thesis, California State University, Los Angeles.

Michalski, K. B., & Guile, M. N. (1990). Readability of state question ballots affects voting behavior. *Bulletin of the Psychonomic Society, 28,* 239–240.

Miller, S. E., Leinhardt, G., & Zigmond, N. (1988). Influencing engagement through accommodation: An ethnographic study of at-risk students. *American Educational Research Journal, 25,* 465–487.

Morawetz, D. (1989). Behavioral self-help treatment for insomnia: A controlled evaluation. *Behavior Therapy, 20,* 365–379.

Motlagh, H. (1968). *Selected non-academic factors related to creativity.* Doctoral dissertation, The University of Tennessee. (University Microfilms no. 68-15,425).

Munger, G. F., & Loyd, B. H. (1989). Gender and attitudes toward computers and calculators: Their relationship to math performance. *Journal of Educational Computing Research, 5,* 167–177.

Nagel, J. J., Himle, D. P., & Papsdorf, J. D. (1989). Cognitive-behavioral treatment of musical performance anxiety. *Psychology of Music, 17,* 12–21.

Nuttall, E. V., Chieh, L., & Nuttall, R. L. (1988). Views of the family by Chinese and U.S. children: A comparative study of kinetic family drawings. *Journal of School Psychology, 26,* 191–194.

Pajak, E. F., & Blase, J. J. (1984). Teachers in bars: From professional to personal self. *Sociology of Education, 57,* 164–173.

Pena, S. T. (1986). *A comparison of the reading attitudes of first-graders in a read aloud tutorial program using trade books and basal readers.* Unpublished master's thesis, California State University, Los Angeles.

Pultzer, E. (1988). Work life, family life, and women's support of feminism. *American Sociological Review, 53,* 640–649.

Reider, M. (1987). *The validity of telephone reports in clinical follow-ups: Follow-ups of former participants in a weight reduction program.* Unpublished master's thesis, California State University, Los Angeles.

Schinke, S. P., Gordon, A. N., & Weston, R. E. (1990). Self-instruction to prevent HIV infection among African-American and Hispanic-American Adolescents. *Journal of Consulting and Clinical Psychology, 58,* 432–436.

Schoenholtz, S. W., Horowitz, H. A., & Shtarkshall, R. (1989). Sex education for emotionally disturbed adolescents. *Journal of Youth and Adolescence, 18,* 97–106.

Smylie, M. A. (1988). The enhancement function of staff development: Organizational and psychological antecedents to individual teacher change. *American Educational Research Journal, 25,* 1–30.

Spiegel, T. A., Wadden, T. A., & Foster, G. D. (1991). Objective measurement of eating rate during behavioral treatment of obesity. *Behavior Therapy, 22,* 61–67.

Stodolsky, S. S., Salk, S., & Glaessner, B. (1991). Student views about learning math and social studies. *American Educational Research Journal, 28,* 89–116.

Telch, C., Agras, W. S., Rossiter, E. M., Wilfley, D., & Kenardy, J. (1990). Group cognitive-behavioral treatment for the nonpurging bulimic: An initial evaluation. *Journal of Consulting and Clinical Psychology, 58,* 629–635.

Trujillo, C. M. (1986). A comparative examination of classroom interactions between professors and minority and non-minority college students. *American Educational Research Journal, 23,* 629–642.

Tuck, D. L., Bayliss, V. A., & Bell, M. L. (1985). Analysis of sex stereotyping in characters created by young authors. *Journal of Educational Research, 78,* 248–252.

Ward, D. A. (1987). Self-esteem and dishonest behavior revisited. *The Journal of Social Psychology, 126,* 709–713.

Ware, N. C., & Lee, V. E. (1988). Sex differences in choice of college science majors. *American Educational Research Journal, 25,* 593–614.

Warren, K. C., & Johnson, R. W. (1989). Family environment, affect, ambivalence and decisions about unplanned pregnancy. *Adolescence, 24,* 505–522.

Weber, C. A. (1986). *A proposed psychological training model incorporating course assessment and attitudes of deans and chairpersons in schools of law and psychology.* Unpublished master's thesis, California State University, Los Angeles.

Wood, J. M., & Bootzin, R. R. (1990). The prevalence of nightmares and their independence from anxiety. *Journal of Abnormal Psychology, 99,* 64–68.

NOTES

Appendix A

CHECKLIST OF PRINCIPLES

Instructors may wish to refer to the following checklist numbers when commenting on students' papers (e.g., "See Principle 5.2.").

Chapter 1: Writing Simple Research Hypotheses

___ 1.1 A simple research hypothesis should name two variables and indicate the type of relationship expected between them.

___ 1.2 When a relationship is expected only among a certain type of subject, reference to the population should be made in the hypothesis.

___ 1.3 A simple hypothesis should be as specific as possible yet expressed in a single sentence.

___ 1.4 If a comparison is to be made, the elements to be compared should be stated.

___ 1.5 Because most hypotheses deal with the behavior of groups, plural forms usually should be used.

___ 1.6 A hypothesis should be free of terms and phrases that do not add to its meaning.

___ 1.7 A hypothesis should indicate what will actually be studied—not the possible implications of the study or value judgments of the author.

___ 1.8 A hypothesis usually should name variables in the order in which they occur or will be measured.

___ 1.9 Avoid using the words "significant" or "significance" in a hypothesis.

___ 1.10 Avoid using the word "prove" in a hypothesis.

___ 1.11 Avoid using two different terms to refer to the same variable.

Chapter 2: A Closer Look at Hypotheses

___ 2.1 A "statement of the hypotheses" may contain more than one hypothesis. It is permissible to include them in a single sentence as long as the sentence is reasonably concise and its meaning is clear.

___ 2.2 When a number of related hypotheses are to be stated, consider presenting them in a numbered or lettered list.

___ 2.3 The hypothesis or hypotheses should be placed before the section on methods.

___ 2.4 It is permissible to use terms other than the term "hypothesis" to refer to a hypothesis. (Use "hypothesis" in term projects, theses, and dissertations.)

___ 2.5 The degree of specificity required in a hypothesis depends on the context in which the hypothesis is presented.

___ 2.6 A hypothesis may be stated without indicating the type of relationship expected between variables. To qualify as a hypothesis, however, it must specify that some unknown type of relationship is expected.

___ 2.7 When a researcher has a research hypothesis, it should be stated in the research paper; the null hypothesis does not always need to be stated (except when required in term projects, theses, and dissertations.)

___ 2.8 Avoid using the word "significant" in the statement of the null hypothesis.

Chapter 3: Writing Research Purposes, Objectives, and Questions

___ 3.1 When the goal of research is to describe group(s) without describing relationships among variables, state a research purpose or question instead of a hypothesis.

___ 3.2 When there is insufficient evidence to permit formulation of a hypothesis regarding a relationship between variables, state a research purpose or question.

___ 3.3 A research purpose or question should be as specific as possible, yet stated concisely.

___ 3.4 When a number of related purposes or questions are to be stated, the author should consider presenting them in a numbered or lettered list.

___ 3.5 The adequacy of a purpose or question should be evaluated in light of the context in which it is stated.

Chapter 4: Writing Titles

___ 4.1 If only a small number of variables are studied, the title should name the variables.

___ 4.2 If many variables are studied, only the *types* of variables should be named.

___ 4.3 The title of a journal article should be concise; the title of a thesis or dissertation may be longer.

___ 4.4 A title should indicate what was studied—not the results of the study.

___ 4.5 Mention the population(s) in a title when the type(s) of population(s) are important.

___ 4.6 Consider the use of subtitles to amplify the purposes or methods of study.

___ 4.7 A title may be stated in the form of a question; this form should be used sparingly and with caution.

___ 4.8 Use the words "effect" and "influence" in titles with caution.

___ 4.9 A title should be consistent with the research hypothesis, purpose, or question.

Chapter 5: Writing Introductions and Literature Reviews

___ 5.1 Start the introduction by describing the problem area; gradually shift its focus to specific research hypotheses, purposes, or questions.

___ 5.2 The significance of a topic should be explicitly stated in the introduction to a term paper, thesis, or dissertation.

___ 5.3 A statement of significance should be specific to the topic investigated.

___ 5.4 Use of the first person is acceptable; it should be used when it facilitates the smooth flow of the introduction.

___ 5.5 The literature review should be presented in the form of an essay — not in the form of an annotated list.

___ 5.6 The literature review should emphasize findings of previous research — not just the methodologies and variables studied.

___ 5.7 Point out trends and themes in the literature.

___ 5.8 Point out gaps in the literature.

___ 5.9 Use the literature review to establish the need for the current study.

___ 5.10 The author should feel free to express opinions about the quality and importance of the research being cited.

___ 5.11 The literature review for a journal article should be highly selective; the review for a thesis or dissertation may be less selective.

___ 5.12 Peripheral research may be cited in a thesis or dissertation when no literature with a direct bearing on the research topic exists. The writer should call the reader's attention to the peripheral nature of the citations.

___ 5.13 Use direct quotations sparingly in literature reviews.

___ 5.14 Report sparingly the details of the literature being cited.

Chapter 6: Writing Definitions

___ 6.1 All of the variables in a research hypothesis, purpose, or question should be defined.

___ 6.2 A defining attribute of a population (also called a control variable) should be defined.

___ 6.3 Theories and models on which a thesis or dissertation are based should be formally defined. In a journal article, the author may choose to provide an informal definition and refer the reader to a publication in which it is described in detail.

___ 6.4 Conceptual definitions should be specific.

___ 6.5 Operational definitions should be provided. These are usually stated in the method section of a report or proposal.

___ 6.6 If a published instrument was used, the variable measured by that instrument may be operationally defined by citing the reference for it.

___ 6.7 If an unpublished instrument was used, the whole instrument should be reproduced in the report or a source for a copy of the instrument should be provided in order to define operationally the variable that was measured.

___ 6.8 Operational definitions should be sufficiently specific so that another investigator can replicate a study with confidence that he or she is examining the same variables under the same circumstances.

___ 6.9 Even a highly operational definition may not be a useful definition.

Chapter 7: Writing Assumptions and Limitations

___ 7.1 In the statement of an assumption, consider stating the reason(s) why it was necessary to make the assumption.

___ 7.2 If there is a reason for believing an assumption is true, state the reason.

___ 7.3 If an assumption is highly questionable, consider casting it as a limitation.

___ 7.4 Consider speculating on the possible effects of a limitation on the results of the study.

___ 7.5 When space permits, be specific in a statement of limitations.

___ 7.6 Consider describing the two types of limitations (i.e., "weaknesses" and "boundaries,") in separate sections or paragraphs. Refer to the first one as "limitations" and the second one as "delimitations."

Chapter 8: Writing Method Sections

___ 8.1 The subjects should be described in enough detail so that the reader can visualize the subjects.

___ 8.2 When the sample is very small, consider providing a description of individual subjects.

___ 8.3 A population should be named and the method used to select the sample should be described.

___ 8.4 If there was attrition, state the number of subjects who dropped out, the reasons for the attrition, if known, and information about the drop-outs, if available.

___ 8.5 If an unpublished instrument was used, describe it in detail.

___ 8.6 If a published instrument was used, briefly describe the traits that it was designed to measure, its format, and the possible range of score values.

___ 8.7 In theses and dissertations, information on reliability and validity should be summarized; in journal articles, it is usually sufficient to refer to a published source of information on these topics if the instrument is well-known and in widespread use.

___ 8.8 Experimental procedures, equipment, and other mechanical matters should be described in sufficient detail so that the study can be replicated.

Chapter 9: Writing Analysis and Results Sections

___ 9.1 Organize the analysis and results section around the research hypotheses (or purposes or questions) stated in the introduction; describe the analysis and results for the first hypothesis first, then describe them for the second hypothesis, and so on.

___ 9.2 Standard statistical procedures need only be named; you do not need to show the formulas.

___ 9.3 Raw scores are usually not reported; only the statistics based on them are reported.

___ 9.4 Present descriptive statistics first, usually starting with measures of central tendency and variability (or, for categorical data, starting with frequencies and percentages).

___ 9.5 Organize large amounts of data in tables and give each table a number and descriptive title (i.e., caption).

___ 9.6 In the text, describe the main conclusions to be reached based on each table and point out highlights that the reader may otherwise overlook. You do not need to discuss each entry in a table.

___ 9.7 Statistical figures (i.e., drawings such as histograms) should be professionally drawn and used sparingly in journal articles.

___ 9.8 Statistical symbols should be underlined or italicized.

___ 9.9 Use the proper case for each statistical symbol.

_____ 9.10 Numerals that start sentences and that are less than 10 should usually be spelled out. (The major exceptions are when referring to an element in a numbered list and when reporting precise numerical results.)

_____ 9.11 Qualitative results need to be organized and the organization made clear to the reader.

Chapter 10: Writing Discussion Sections

_____ 10.1 A brief summary of the study may be included in the discussion section of a journal article; a longer, formal summary may be required in a thesis or dissertation.

_____ 10.2 If hypotheses were stated in the introduction, it is usually appropriate to restate them and indicate whether they were supported by the data.

_____ 10.3 Highlights of the results should be described in the discussion section.

_____ 10.4 When possible, explicitly state the implications of the results in the discussion section.

_____ 10.5 Important strengths and limitations should be mentioned in the discussion section.

_____ 10.6 If you issue a call for further research on a problem, provide the reader with specific guidance.

_____ 10.7 Point out consistencies and inconsistencies of the current results with those in the literature cited earlier in the report.

_____ 10.8 It is acceptable to speculate on the meaning of the results.

_____ 10.9 It is usually inappropriate to introduce new data or new references to literature in the discussion and conclusion section.

Chapter 11: Writing Abstracts

_____ 11.1 Highlights of the results usually should be included in the abstract.

_____ 11.2 Highlights of the methodology usually should be mentioned.

_____ 11.3 Reference to the research purposes, questions, or hypotheses usually should be made.

_____ 11.4 The abstract for a journal article usually should be a single paragraph.

Appendix B

THINKING STRAIGHT AND WRITING THAT WAY*

Ann Robinson

University of Arkansas at Little Rock

Everyone who submits manuscripts to top-flight journals gets rejected by the reviewers more than once in his or her publishing career. Often the rejections seem at best inexplicable and at worst biased. Rejections sting.

In a cooler moment, the disappointed author looks over the rejected paper and tries to read the reviewers' comments more calmly. What do journal reviewers look for in a manuscript? What makes a submission publishable? How can you increase the likelihood that your work will be accepted? These are good questions for any would-be author—seasoned or new—to ask.

In general, sessions on publishing "how-to's" rarely get beyond the obligatory lecture on the importance of the idea. We are told that if the idea is good, we should carry out the research study and proceed to submit the work for publication. If the how-to-get-published session gets past the point of explaining that a good study is one that asks an important question, then we are told that a publishable study is one that is reasonably free of design flaws. It seems to me that these two points ought to be considered givens. Although it is not always easy to think of a good idea, translate it into a researchable question, and design a competent study, most of us already understand the importance of these things. What we want to know *now* is how to increase our chances of getting competent work published.

Over the last eight years, I have developed the following questions to use when reviewing research manuscripts. They are offered as

*Originally published in *Gifted Child Quarterly, 32,* 367-369, as "Thinking Straight and Writing That Way: Publishing in *Gifted Child Quarterly.*" Copyright 1988 by the National Association for Gifted Children. Reprinted with permission.

one reviewer's "test" of the publishability of a manuscript and may be helpful as guides for the prospective author.

Reviewer Question 1: What's the point?

Early on in the first "quick read," I ask why I should be interested in this manuscript. Will this study fill a gap in the existing literature? Will this study reconcile apparently contradictory research results from studies already published? Is this study anchored to a real problem affecting the education and upbringing of children and youth? Is this study "newsworthy?" Does the author convince me in the first few paragraphs that this manuscript is going to present important information new to the field or be investigated from a fresh perspective?

The manuscripts which most effectively make their "point" often have brief introductions which state the essence of the issue in the first or last sentence of the first or second paragraph. As a reviewer, I look for that "essence of issue" sentence. It is a bench mark for clear thinking and writing.

Reviewer Question 2: Can I find the general research question?

Reviewer Question 2 is related to the first, but I am now looking for something a bit more technical. The general research question should be stated clearly, and it should serve as the lodestone for the specific questions generated for the study. Congruence is important here. If I were to take each of these specific questions and check them against the general question, I would easily see the connection. For example, in a study of the family systems of underachieving males, the general question is, "What are the interactional relationships within families of gifted students?" (Green, Fine, & Tollefson, 1988). Two specific questions derived from the general one are:

"(1) Is there a difference in the proportion of families of achieving and underachieving gifted that are classified as functional and dysfunctional?

(2) Do family members having achieving or underachieving gifted students differ in their satisfaction with their families?" (p. 268).

The manuscripts which most effectively answer Reviewer Question 2 placed the general question at the end of the review of the literature. It will be stated as a question and prefaced with a lead-in like "the general purpose of this study" or "an important research question is." Then the specific questions for the study are enumerated and set apart in a list. The combination of text and visual cues makes it difficult for the reviewer to overlook the focus of the manuscript.

Reviewer Question 3: Can I get a "picture" of the subjects of this study?

The appropriate level of description for the subjects is difficult to judge. However, it is better to over- rather than underdescribe them. This is true whether the study is experimental or a naturalistic inquiry. Insufficient information about the participants in the study leaves the reviewer wondering if the conclusions are suspect. Would the results be the same if other subjects had participated? Go beyond the breakdowns by age or grade, sex, and ethnicity. If the subjects are students in a gifted program, describe the identification procedure. If the subjects are school personnel, describe their professional positions, years in service, or other variables which might affect the results. As a reviewer, I always try to determine the extent to which a subject sample is volunteer and how seriously volunteerism might bias the results. If a study is conducted in one school building, district, or one teacher or parent advocate group, I look for descriptions of this context. How large is the school or organization? Is it rural, urban, or suburban? Who is responding to surveys? Fathers or mothers? Are families intact, single parent, or extended? What is the socioeconomic level?

For example, in a study of learning styles, Ricca (1984) included the following information to give a thorough picture of the subjects.

The study population included 425 students in grades four, five and six from one city school and one suburban school district in Western New York. Descriptive contrast groups represented subjects who were identified as gifted and a contrast group taken from the remaining general school students available. Gifted students were identified by a multidimensional screening process with data sources indicated in Table 1 (p. 121).

This information is followed by a further explanation of the identification process and three brief tables which provide a tidy summary of student demographics and cognitive and academic characteristics. The combination of text and tables gives the reviewer a clear picture of the subjects in the study.

The reviewer may ultimately ask the author to trim the text on subjects, but over-zealous descriptions serve two purposes. First they demonstrate to the reviewer that the author is a careful worker. Second, they rein in generalizations which appear in the Conclusions and Implications sections of the manuscript. An author may well be entitled to make statements about the population from which the sample of subjects is drawn, but if the demographics of the group change, the conclusions may not be safely generalized.

The manuscripts which most effectively create a picture of their sample include the basics like age, grade, sex, and ethnicity succinctly, sometimes in tabled form. Case study researchers are less likely to use tables because of smaller samples, but they do identify the reasons why they believe a subject is representative of a large group. In studies of gifted children the most effective manuscripts clearly state the selection procedure and identify specific instruments or checklists, if appropriate, under the Subjects section of the paper.

Reviewer Question 4: Is this author killing flies with an elephant gun?

As a reviewer, I examine the manuscript for a comfortable fit among the research questions, the kinds of data that have been collected, and the tools of analysis. In the case of manuscripts which present quantitative data and statistical analyses, I apply Occam's razor. The simplest statistics are usually the best. A good research question can be insightfully investigated with relatively simple analyses provided the assumptions are not too badly violated. The purpose of statistics is to summarize and clarify, not to fog.

Of course, authors who seek to control confounded variables through the use of more sophisticated statistical treatments like the currently popular LISREL increase the likelihood that multiple causation is disentangled. We certainly gain from technological innovation; however, the key is to determine if the impetus for the study is a substantive research question or a fascination with the newest techniques.

The manuscripts which answer Reviewer Question 4 most effectively are those in which hypotheses do not sink under the weight of the analyses. As I read the Design and Analysis sections, am I able to keep my eye on the important variables? A good indicator is a sentence in the Design section which gives me the rationale for using quite sophisticated or new statistical and qualitative techniques.

For example, a study of ethnic differences in a mathematics program for gifted students included the following explanation for the selection of a specialized kind of regression analysis (Robinson, Bradley, & Stanley, in review):

> Regression discontinuity is a quasi-experimental design which allows the experimenter to test for treatment effects without a randomized control group and the attendant withholding of services. This a priori design statistically controls for prior differences by using the identification variable along with program participation (status) as independent variables in a multiple regression model (p.7).

Another indication that the study is being driven by its questions rather than its statistics is the author's effort to make connecting statements between a technique and its interpretation. To return to the previous regression example:

> If the associated t-test of the regression coefficient is significant, it is indicative of a program that impacts on its participants (p. 7).

Reviewer Question 5: Would George Orwell approve?

Dogging the reviewer through both the "quick read" and the "close read" of the manuscript is the ease with which the author has answered the first four questions. If we look back at those questions, we see the common thread of clarity running through them. What is the point? Where is the question? Who is this study about? Does the analysis illuminate rather than obfuscate?

Reviewer Question 5 is the final test. Would George Orwell approve? In 1946 Orwell published "Politics and the English Language," one of the clearest statements on writing effectively ever to appear in print. The thesis of his essay was that "modern English, especially written English, is full of bad habits which spread by imitation and which can be avoided if one is willing to take the necessary trouble . . . prose consists less and less of *words* chosen for the sake of their meaning, and more and more of *phrases* tacked together like sections of a prefabricated hen-house" (p. 159). Orwell was clearly unhappy with vague writing and professional jargon. He felt that poor writing was an indication of sloppy thinking, and he excused neither the social scientist nor the novelist from his strict dicta of good, vigorous writing. He had a particular dislike of using ready-made phrases like "lay the foundation," and he was equally appalled at the indiscriminate use of scientific terms to give the impression of objectivity to biased statements.

As a reviewer, I apply Orwell's tough rules to the test of every manuscript I receive. It means that the manuscript author has answered Reviewer Questions 1 through 4 successfully.

According to Orwell, "the following rules will cover most cases:

1. Never use a metaphor, simile or other figure of speech which you are used to seeing in print.
2. Never use a long word where a short one will do.
3. If it is possible to cut a word out, always cut it out.
4. Never use the passive where you can use the active.
5. Never use a foreign phrase, a scientific word or a jargon word if you can think of an everyday English equivalent.
6. Break any of these rules sooner than say anything outright barbarous" (p. 170).

Orwell has the good sense to include the sixth rule as a disclaimer. All writers make errors and violate rules, sometimes out of carelessness, sometimes for effect. It is also true that writing for highly specialized journals does require the judicious use of technical language, just as sheep shearers need specialized terms to describe differing grades of wool. However, moderation in the use and the arbitrary, spontaneous creation of specialized vocabulary is certainly warranted in our field. It is refreshing to read an author who states that the subjects in the study are "thinking critically" rather than "realizing greater cognitive gains."

Orwell makes many fine points about the importance of sincerity in thinking and writing. For the prospective social science writer, none is more important than the careful selection and lively use of technical terms. I know of no more rigorous test to apply to a manuscript than to ask if George Orwell would approve. Passing this "test" means the author is thinking straight and writing that way.

References

Green, K., Fine, M. J., & Tollefson, N. (1988). Family systems characteristics and underachieving gifted adolescent males. *Gifted Child Quarterly, 32,* 267-276.

Orwell, G. (1953). Politics and the English language. In G. Orwell (Ed.), *A collection of essays* (pp. 156-171). San Diego: Harcourt, Brace, Jovanovich.

Rica, J. (1984). Learning styles and preferred instructional strategies. *Gifted Child Quarterly, 28,* 121-126.

Robinson, A., Bradley, R. & Stanley, T.D. (in review). Opportunity to achieve: The identification and performance of black students in a program for the mathematically talented.

NOTES

FUNDAMENTAL PRINCIPLES FOR PREPARING PSYCHOLOGY JOURNAL ARTICLES*

Harry F. Harlow

University of Wisconsin

As retiring Editor of the *Journal of Comparative and Physiological Psychology,* I feel that I have one remaining responsibility to my psychological colleagues. Having passed judgment on about 2,500 original manuscripts and almost as many revisions in my 12 years as Editor, I believe I should bequeath to posterity some principles of scientific reporting that I have formulated only through countless hours of moonlighting.

Covering Letter

In plotting the publication of a manuscript the prospective author should think first about the covering letter. It is an unforgivable error to write, "I am submitting a manuscript for your consideration . . . ." This evasive method gets you nowhere with editors. Even if the nondirective technique works with many patients, there are some sick people who are best approached using positive pressures.

There are a number of general principles underlying a good covering letter, and they can by illustrated by example. I offer the following:

Dear Harry:

I am submitting the manuscript, "Creative Thinking by Paramecia," for publication in *JCPP*. My chairman has assured me that upon acceptance of this manuscript he will recommend me for promotion to associate professor. Two recipients of the Distinguished Psychologist Award have reviewed this paper and

---

*Reprinted from Harlow, H. F. (1962). *Journal of Comparative and Physiological Psychology, 55,* 893-896.

recommend it highly.

I am pleased to see that you are one of the five candidates for President of the American Psychological Association. As you know, I have nominated you for many years and will probably give you my support in the future.

Because of the unusual significance of these researches, I would like early publication, which I will finance from my National Institute of Mental Health grant.

Warm regards,

John Hopeful
Assistant Professor

The battle is now half won. You will get a fair shake.

Introduction

Almost all scientific papers include an introduction even though large parts of it are frequently buried in the sections labeled Method and Results. However, the total omission of an introduction constitutes a glaring error, and, anyway, it is fun to write introductions—one is not constrained by facts.

One way to write an introduction is simply to state what the experiment is all about and make predictions about the outcome. Since the data will already have been collected and processed, you will have no difficulty in making insightful predictions. As all famous historians know, one can predict the past with great precision. However, prediction is one of the great booby traps into which young and inexperienced psychologists often fall. All their predictions are confirmed; older men know that this never happens. The proper technique is to select the prediction of minimum import, or throw in a completely extraneous one, and have this prediction fail. Honesty is the best policy.

Although some psychologists write simple, straightforward introductions, this is commonly considered to be *declasse*. In the sophisticated or "striptease" technique you keep the problem a secret from the reader until the very last paragraph. Indeed, some very sophisticated authors keep the problem a secret forever. Since I am interested in readers as well as authors, I advise that readers always approach introduction sections using the Chinese technique—begin at the end and read backward.

104

The function of the introduction is to impress your colleagues with your scholarship and erudition—academic appointments are seldom made on the basis of a results section. Scholarly one-upmanship is attained with an unending number of nonspecific references, such as:

"The up-and-down effect was first discovered by (_____, 1762) and this study led to many fruitful investigations (_____, 1804; _____, 1827; _____, 1844; _____, 1861; _____, 1874; _____, 1888; _____ 1894; _____ 1911; _____ 1917; _____ 1928; _____, 1937; _____, 1944; and _____ 1952). Beyond these researches the broad implications of this discovery led to related studies on the in-and-out phenomenon (_____, 1829; _____, 1855; _____, 1888; _____, 1914; _____, 1927; and _____, 1950), and the around-and-about law (_____, 1884; _____, 1914; _____, 1933; _____, 1947; _____, 1952; and _____, 1960)."

Often, but not often enough, young and lazy authors are frightened away from this technique simply because they are appalled by the amount of work involved in reading the literature, especially if part is written in some foreign language. However, there is no excuse for this attitude; the author should remember that he is not reading the literature—just citing it. Anyway, he can always rely on some scholarly article in *Psychological Bulletin* as a secondary source to provide an impressive reference list with almost no effort.

Occasionally editors object to overly extended, striptease introductions and to long lists of nonspecific references. At this point the author should take the bull by the horns and write the editor a nasty letter accusing him of rigidity, illiteracy, and lack of scholarly interests. Editors are busy and editors are human. They can be broken—don't pamper them.

Method

To write a good Method section, one must be an idealist. If this section is to be understood, it must be clear, orderly, and systematic. The best way to achieve this is not to tell what really happened, or if you must tell, wait as long as is physically possible. Your four groups of *Ss* should always add to 20 or 30 each. If 7 *Ss* in Group 2 died of pneumonia and 19 *Ss* in Group 3 were suffocated, don't put it in the Method section. The death of these *Ss* was not planned but resulted, and the information obviously belongs in the Results. There is also good reason for putting this information in the Discussion because you can then mediate on how different the results might have been had the *Ss* lived.

A mechanical problem that often creeps up in Method relates to the spelling and meaning of words such as "maize," "liman," and "maccaccuss resus." Fortunately there is a fundamental rule. Writing manuscripts is a tedious process and time means money. You must protect your time in every possible manner. If you cannot spell or do not know the meaning of a word, don't look it up in *Webster's Third International Dictionary.* If the word isn't in Thorndike and Barnhart, 95% of your psychological audience won't know the meaning of the word or how to spell it anyway. Moreover, that's the Editor's responsibility. Let well enough alone.

Results

The Results section comes in a very convenient place, and one way to start it is to put the procedures which you inadvertently omitted from the Method section—which you are too lazy to rewrite—at the very beginning of the Results.

If the Editor objects, point out that you are doing this for the sake of continuity. The next problem can only be resolved by reference to the Procedure. Reread the Procedure section and find out the order that you said you were going to follow; then, carefully rearrange that order in the Results. If you write succinctly and clearly, there is a real danger that the reader will only read your manuscript once, and every psychologist worth his salt recognizes the importance of overlearning. Then, too, if he has to struggle to understand it, he will naturally attribute the difficulties to the abstruseness of the problem.

The most important items in the Results will probably be the figures. Authors seldom realize the importance of figures and consequently fail to give them sufficient attention. It is absolutely imperative that the figures be of professional quality. This may cost a little money, but even with academic salaries what they are, the cost is cheap compared with the value of the man-hours spent in gathering and processing the data. The ordinate and abscissa should be boldly drawn and the curves should stand out like sore thumbs, which they frequently really are.

Now we are at a critical point. It is important to make sure that all legends, all numbers on the ordinate and abscissa, and all titles are completely unreadable. If you fail to do this, there is a real danger that editors and readers will compare the information given in the graph with what is written in the Results and Discussion and call the discrepancies to your attention. Fortunately your figures can be made unreadable at a high academic level by following a few simple rules. Draw the figure on paper 2 ft. sq. and never purchase templates with letters more than 1/4 in. high. Then when the figures are reduced in size for Journal publication, the data will remain a personal secret. You can subsequently let out the data you are not trying to hide by personal correspondence.

Even authors who follow this rule — and the general principle is widely understood — frequently make a completely unforgivable error by sending glossy prints of their figures to the Editor. If the Editor has already recognized the fact that he has presbyopia and has purchased glasses, he may insist that the graphs be redrawn, and then the jig is up. However, if you send the original drawings and simply scratch out in pencil the copy for the carbon which some editors require, you have a high chance of success. A better technique is to send the carbon without figures. Most editors will relay this carbon to a consulting editor without checking for figures, and a single favorable review frequently insures publication.

Another good technique is to supplement the figures by presenting the data for individual animals in lengthy tables without means, medians, or standard deviations. No reader, and certainly no editor, will ever take the trouble to make the necessary computations to check your curves or statements of significance. The additional advantage is that long, detailed tables carry the implication that you engaged in an overwhelmingly complicated piece of research.

Discussion

Whereas there are firm rules and morals concerning the collection and reporting of data which should be placed in the Results, these rules no longer are in force when one comes to the Discussion. Anything goes—shoot the moon—the sky's the limit!

Even though one is going far afield, the endeavor should not be random, but the deception should be achieved with skill and grace. The most important fundamental guiding principle is to repeat the predictions made in the introduction—elaborating them if possible—and then to describe the importance of your work in broad generic terms and never get down to mundane fact. In Discussion sections one does not discover things about maze performance, minutes to run down a straight alley, 48 hr. of food deprivation, or the number of mechanical puzzle devices opened—one makes breath-taking discoveries about learning, drive reduction, motivation, and curiosity. After all, this is the way psychologists are going to talk when they present and discuss their work at scientific meetings, and no man attains fluency in the jargon without practice.

Very occasionally some psychologist makes the mistake of saying what is worth saying in the Discussion and then stopping. This is interpreted by other psychologists as indicating that the person lacks verbal skill and creativity. Anyone can talk effectively about data which actually exist.

If your experiment has any merit whatsoever, and little is required, there is the likelihood that someone else will do it later and do it better. To save face it is important to engage in the alibi-in-advance technique. Endless Discussion pages can be consumed by describing how you would do the experiment if you were to do it over, and the joy of this device is that no data need be collected. You have the fellow who is going to be so cold and calculating as to check your results, on the run, and if you are smart enough, no matter what he obtains, it will be a dry run.

Even if you have only completed a single experiment you can greatly augment your data by several pages of descriptions of the results you would have obtained had you done a long series of related experiments. Furthermore, a clarity is achieved by describing the experiments that were not done instead of those that were because the results in the imaginary experiments come out in an integrated, orderly manner that is seldom achieved in the laboratory. Remember that data collection is a routine process and the brilliant scientist will rise above it when he comes to the Discussion.

Nothing is now left except to find a way to end the Discussion section, which has become so long and so confused that most readers will have forgotten what the original problem was about anyway. Discussion should be concluded in a friendly, charitable, and slightly condescending manner. First, say a few little things about the difficulties of doing research, particularly research in your chosen area. Then point out that there are a few little technical problems and research odds and ends that need to be picked up before your area of choice is completely neat and tidy. Finally, explain that once the research trail has been broken, less strong bodies can follow along.

Footnotes

Finally, one comes to the footnotes. Footnotes are always on a separate page (or pages) and there is a chance that the Editor will miss them, particularly if the typewritten material is single-spaced and turned upside down. Thus, here is an opportunity to introduce a couple of additional pages of complete trivia. If the Editor should discover them, nothing will be lost, for paper is cheap. Remember that this is your last chance to get in some padding, and never forget the fact that promotion is the prerogative of deans and final decisions are frequently weighed on other scales than those of justice.

Special attention should be given to one footnote—the acknowledgement. It is this one that separates the men from the boys. Since most experiments are not worth doing and the data obtained are not worth publishing, great care should be taken to protect one's reputation when one's name is associated with the conventional potboiler. This can be achieved by a simple and honest footnote.

"The author (or authors) had very little to do with this research. The idea was stolen from Dr. _____, the experimental design was proposed by my (our) statistical consultant, Dr. _____, the *Ss* were run by Mr. _____ and Miss _____, the data were processed by the mathematical computing center, and the paper was completely rewritten by Editor _____, on the basis of extensive notes and suggestions made by Consulting Editor _____, whose name was inadvertently left off the masthead of the *Journal of* _____.

Editorial Policy

Faced with a mounting flood of uninspired researches and watching publication lag continuously mount despite multiple allotments of additional *Journal* pages, I came to realize that my editorial policies, even though rigid and unreasonable, were incomplete or else in error. For a long time I thought there was no solution, and then I realized that I was wrong. I established a new *JCPP* policy and formalized it with a rubber stamp, only to realize that my term as Editor had already expired. But at least I have the rubber stamp which I planned to use on a large number of manuscripts: "Not read but rejected."

Appendix D

SUGGESTED READINGS, SOFTWARE, AND VIDEOTAPES

American Educational Research Association (1991). *Professional publishing in professional journals.* Washington, DC: Author.

A set of two tapes, containing panel discussions on professional publishing. Includes topics such as style, selecting a journal, and how to respond to reviewers and editors.

American Psychological Association (1990). *Journals in psychology: A resource listing for authors.* Washington, DC: Author.

Provides information on 280 periodicals in the social and behavioral sciences, including editorial policies and notes on submissions.

American Psychological Association (1983). *Publication manual of the American Psychological Association.* (3rd ed.) Washington, DC: Author.

An important reference for those who write for journals of the American Psychological Association (APA). Includes a chapter on the expression of ideas that all students should find of value. Most education journals require that authors follow either this style manual or the *Chicago Manual of Style*, which is described below.

Baumann, J. F., & Johnson, D. D. (1991). *Writing for publication in reading and language arts.* Newark, DE: International Reading Association.

Describes basic information on writing for publication. The first four chapters present the views of four authors on writing for journals in reading and language arts.

111

Hensen, K. T. (1988). Writing for education journals. *Phi Delta Kappan, 69,* 752-754.

Lists important characteristics of 49 education journals. Of special interest to writers are acceptance rates, average number of weeks required for a decision, and preferred length of manuscripts.

Oberon Resources (1990-91). *WP citation.* Columbus, OH: Author.

A bibliographic citation computer program for use with the popular WordPerfect word processing program. It generates reference citations in various publication styles after the user has entered bibliographic information such as authors' names, titles, pages, and dates.

Richardson, M., & Prickett, R. (1991). *Publication sources for educational leadership.* Lancaster, PA: Technomic Publishing Company.

Lists more than 300 journals for that publish education articles. Describes journals and provides contact information.

University of Chicago Press (1982). *The Chicago manual of style.* (13th ed.). Chicago: Author.

Describes standards for style required by many education journals. An important reference for all students of the social and behavioral sciences.